Be Relevant!
How Brands Rise To The Top

A Practical Guide to Service Design

(Non-Profit Edition)

Be Relevant!

How Brands Rise To The Top

A Practical Guide to Service Design

(Non-Profit Edition)

by

Steven J. Slater

Copyright

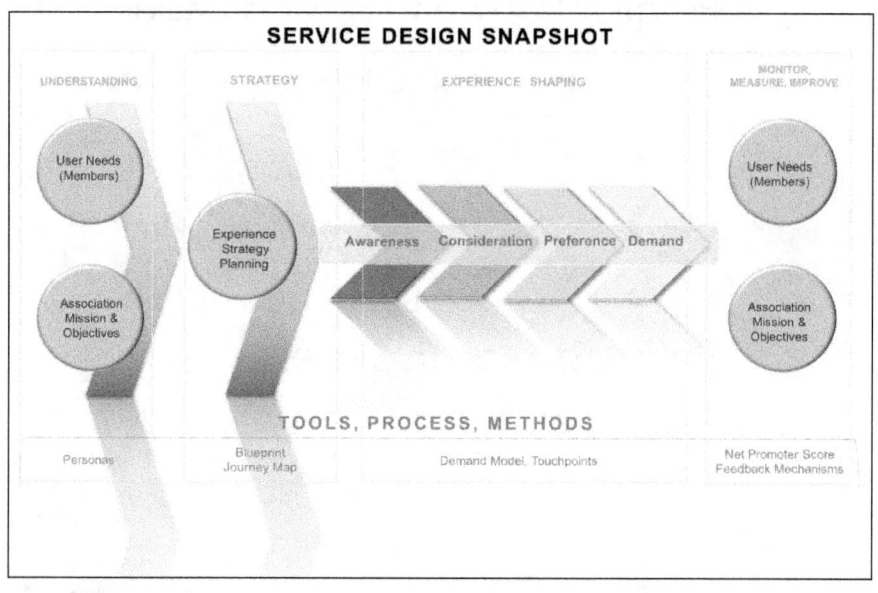

Dedication

To those who have mentored me over the years and to those who consider me their mentor.

You have all shaped the person I have become... *hopefully for the better.*

Table of Contents

Introduction

"You may not have heard of service design yet, but I'd argue that it's the most important design subspecialty in the business world today."
—Kerry Bodine, Forester analyst

Service Design is not a synonym for Graphic Design, Web Usability and Metrics, User Experiences, Customer Service, Design Thinking, or Industrial Design. Rather, Service Design is none of these disciplines, but at any given time a service designer could find it useful to borrow from them, including tools, models, methods, and best practices. Service Design is a practice for organizing people, process, and technology for successful services.

A successful service, meantime, is one that reliably and repeatedly creates unique, individual, positive experiences. In the hands of a properly skilled service designer, "Service Design will dramatically improve the productivity and quality of services," according to its definition on Wikipedia.

In my thirty years designing services, what some refer to as developing Lines of Service (LOS), I have found no equivalent field to Service Design. Its techniques and principles have helped me in my work to overcome company and organization challenges, include engaging millennials, create sources of revenue, and ensure long-term sustainability.

However, I came to writing about Service Design after failing to find a prescription that executives, or anyone else, could use to developing their own successful service. I also grew concerned with inconsistencies written about Service Design, and when I came across information I thought could be of value to share, it was often buried or obscured by nonsense.

I have read and heard a body of knowledge exists for Service Design, but after more than a year of knowledge-gathering, it has yet to materialize. I began to conclude, if I didn't attempt to sort it out through some logic and experience, others would give up long before realizing the benefits and value of Service Design. Even worse, I have to admit, my fear is that some will take liberties to fill the voids for their short term gain, that in the long run would misalign the reputation of Service Design.

So, I began by accumulating the models, tools, and methods that have served me well for the past three decades, and then chose a service blueprint as an artificial midpoint in a lifecycle of service development. I then worked backward and forward, cherry-picking from my experiences and fitting in the models where they best fit. As I look over what I have laid out here, I am confident the sequence will lead to successful services.

The objective for any service is one that satisfies the needs of users, and leads to a satisfactory experience — and equally important, meets the needs and objectives of the organization.

I will have succeeded if this guide helps others develop successful services and will also consider this a success if I provoke discussions for the definition of Service Design. Meantime, to those who find the material valuable, I would be pleased to hear from you. I can be reached at steven@steven-jslater.com.

I wish you great fulfillment.

Steven

Prologue

"Service design is the activity of planning and organizing people, infrastructure, communication and material components of a service to improve its quality and the interaction between service provider and customers."

–Wikipedia, Service Design

In the tradition of Italian Renaissance-period Commedia dell'arte—a form of theater popular in Europe for nearly 300 years—no two performances were alike.

Commedia has all the essentials of a well-designed, carefully managed service. The genre followed a predictable formula yet allowed just enough variation so each performance was unique to a community at a point in time.

Troupes of ten to twelve performers roamed towns and villages entertaining audiences with the purpose of creating memorable experiences so the troupe would be invited back. Scouts would run ahead of scheduled stops to learn the names of local officials, get the scoop on gossip, and take note of any peccadillos, all to be used as the basis for roughed-in plots.

Scenes and acts would also change to match their locale and reflect the local audience tolerance and taste. Still, while scripts and scenes helped to keep the performances fresh, audiences anticipated the return of a retinue of personas in familiar roles. These were characters sometimes represented by facially disproportionate, garish masks. Among them were The Fool, The Old Wealthy Merchant, The Charlatan, The Mischievous Maid, and The Braggart Solider, along with about a half-dozen others. Even today, theater history students will be able to recite most these characters.

The success of a performance relied on the performers' ability to connect with their audience—made more difficult while shielded head to toe in bright geometric harlequin-style costumes, exquisite uniforms, and full-length draped robes—besides having their facial expressions hidden behind masks.

LORENZO C. 83

As such, performers used literary devices and physical feats to bring their characters to life. Sometimes these devices were to amuse, other times to provide a break in the action, but mostly to evoke emotion for heightening audience anticipation—all contrived to move skeletal plots to a meaningful conclusion.

When adding new bits into a performance, the performers would look to the audience's reaction to measure whether a particular soliloquy, comedic action, or witty discourse hit the mark. Audience feedback is not unlike a touchpoint, an approach used in Service Design to learn from an audience and improve.

Meantime, notebooks that survived the era, show how performers associated specific acts or actions with audience responses, along with their cues for when to use them.

Troupes were distinguished by their off-stage, on-stage camaraderie. Audiences could spot the differences by how the performers collaborated onstage and their ability to react and improvise off one another. Service Design also promotes an off-stage and on-stage viewpoint in which a service blueprint model helps teams recognize the importance of collaborating and coordinating for ensuring successful service outcomes.

Even with all the formal preparation and contrived familiarity and nuances around each performance—audience satisfaction wrested on relating to the performers as real people. A successful production was one in which performers let the audiences in on the charade. One of the ways this was accomplished: bringing to the stage those real-life situations involving the real people behind the masks, such as celebrating life's milestones and sharing common perils that impact most everyone.

Commedia would appear to embody much of the thinking and wisdom of Service Design. Commedia is in line with Service Design with its focus on satisfying narrow, specific audiences and taking great care to meet their expectations. Additionally, Commedia uses methods that Service Design includes for achieving these aims. These methods include: an overall ridged structure for setting the boundary of acceptability; elements of a service that can change or are altered to suit specific circumstances; feedback mechanisms to learn and improve; and, a mirror approach that services take place onstage and offstage, and the two require coordination.

There have been Commedia troupes formed recently. But given the entertainment alternatives to satisfy our individual needs—including the ability to travel easily, communicate electronically, and stream content in the moment, this genre is likely limited to nostalgia.

Chapter I
The Allure of Service Design

"Design is not just what it looks like and feels like. Design is how it works."

—Steve Jobs

1 – DEPENDING ON QUALITY SERVICES

By the mid-20th century, services began to overtake products in the nation's GDP. Yet unlike industrial design, there was no framework for designing services.

"There is no way to ensure quality or uniformity in the absence of a detailed design," Citibank marketing executive G. Lynn Shostack wrote in 1982 for Harvard Business Review.

"No one systematically quantifies the process or devises tests to ensure that the service is complete, rational, and fulfills the original need," she continued. "No R&D departments, laboratories, or service engineers to define or oversee the design."

Shostack used the article to propose a visual model depicting planned and unforeseen consequences from a user's interaction with a service, which she called a service blueprint. She expressed her hope the blueprint would be used for a common language for all those involved in designing a service.

Her ideas were adopted in Cologne, Germany, by academics who began building a service design practice by adding tools and models. In due time, the practice included methods and approaches borrowed from ethnography, behavioral sciences, human systems integration, sociology, and other fields. But the tipping point for its bona fides was when European Union governments adopted the practice for building and improving public works projects that required common understanding among multi-cultural users.

Service Design proved successful and caught the eye of entrepreneurs, particularly those in the highly-competitive consumer goods sector. Among those who took notice was Steve Jobs, who according to his biographer, began experimenting with Service Design techniques to try and gain leverage in the sales cycle.

SERVICE DESIGN TOOLS	USED FOR	BENEFIT - PURPOSE
PERSONAS	Identify and refine targets by those you desire to influence – group based upon common factors, primarily who share like-mindedness.	Understand target audience needs, motivations, goals, aspirations.
JOURNEY MAPS	Determine messages, communications channels.	How and what to communicate to desired target audience.
DEMAND MODELS	Guide users along a desired path to a decision.	Know and recognize how to influence a decision.
SERVICE BLUEPRINT	Visualize the Service System and Service Operation	For building, repairing, monitoring and improving.
TOUCHPOINTS	Manage the communications operation planned with input from personas, Journey Maps, Demand Models, and Service Blueprint.	Two-way communications – push desired messages, effectively use all-any communications channels, and solicit feedback.

Jobs applied Service Design through the company's customer interactions with the goal of conveying the purpose and feeling behind owning an Apple product. Service Design was used to demonstrate a range of vibrant experiences only possible through Apple. The possibilities emphasized lifestyle enhancements around arts, culture, and music, including better internet browsing, photo editing, movie making, and creating and organizing music.

Today, many market leading companies are using Service Design, even though most of us are not aware or are unable to recognize the techniques. Among them: Amazon, Google, Airbnb, Toyota, Uber, Capital One, Pepsi, Marriott and many more.

The demise of the Ringling Bros. circus was not surprising among some observers. For all one could tell, the performances of late could have resembled shows dating to their inception one hundred and fifty years ago. Meanwhile, one of their competitors, Cirque Du Soleil, is now the largest theatrical producer in the world. They found success tapping into a new market—one of their own creation.

Ringling Bros. ended in May 2017 due to dwindling audiences, the company said in a statement. Owner Ken Feld blamed the closing on the decision to remove elephants from the big tent. A ringleader interviewed on 60-Minutes, offered that he believed today's youth prefers apps and online games to live entertainment.

However, that version does not square with the success by Cirque Du Soleil, which got its start building on concepts and ideas from the Moscow Circus. I remember attending that Circus as a teen, thinking it was unlike any other. Performers would flub and fumble along a cleverly choreographed performance of Russian myths and lore—leading audiences to anticipate a spectacular failure as each trick became increasingly difficult. But of course, at the end the trick came off beautifully, leaving audiences wanting more.

Cirque crafted its performances similarly, with the intent to defy audience expectations. "If you have watched any of its performances you will notice a new definition of a circus," Kelly Luo wrote in an article on her LinkedIn profile. "It was familiar yet strangely new."

Catering to the audience has been the company's mantra since its beginning and is carefully implemented. Audiences are polled on their experiences: from when they first considered attending, to buying a ticket, their journeys to the performance and back, and to learning about their lasting impressions.

Meantime, audience reactions are gauged during performances to assess how performers interact with audiences and any resulting emotions. "The company also solicits ideas from within. Once a year, Cirque assembles its roughly five thousand employees to learn about the shows and ways to improve. These assemblies turn into brainstorming sessions for ways to meet audience needs for the future. The process follows along this path: creative teams accumulate audience and staff input; they sort the feedback and select those ideas that lend themselves to new themes and storylines for upcoming shows. From there, the characters, scenery, and music are crafted to fit.

The performers for new shows depicting characters are only partly based on their skills, talents, and tricks. They are also chosen by audience reactions to them with any emotions they evoke. To that end, Cirque catalogues its performers' traits, stored into a database that is accessible to show directors.

Ultimately, every aspect of every performance is singularly intended to create an unforgettable experience—one that leaves audiences satisfied and hopefully eager to buy tickets for another show. Shows, such as "O," have been selling out at the Bellagio in Las Vegas, NV, for more than fifteen years, where a theater was built just for that performance.

Against this backdrop, one wonders whether Ringling Bros. could have survived. For the entire 20th century the traveling circus was a popular form of family entertainment. It appealed to audiences of all ages for its G-rated content, which at the time were unimaginable feats, including acrobatics and animal tricks; and of course, there were the clowns. In fact, the entire experience was cloaked in a large wink and a nod to its youthful attendees. They certainly knew their audience.

However, one could argue, as did the ringleader, that today's youth have much more stimuli—the breadth, intimacy and affordability of the internet, and the immediacy of communications. Its impact to Ringling cannot be overstated. Their ideal audience was no longer satisfied by a Ringling

Bros. experience. And if the youth were no longer tugging on their parents to take them to the circus, well then, the audience was no longer satisfied going to the circus, year after year. Ringling was forced to close not because elephants were no longer a part—but because the Ringling Bros. circus was no longer filling a need, unable to satisfy an audience in sufficient numbers. The experience was no longer relevant.

Circuses are in our past; they have just merely shifted in a new direction. Through listening to its target audience market, infused with innovation, lively colors, action and contemporary music, Cirque du Soleil thrives. The company earns more than $200 billion a year by selling tickets and merchandise, according to estimates by Dun & Bradstreet. Its shows have been seen by more than 100 million spectators in nearly 300 cities on five continents. It has achieved its success mostly by satisfying an adult target market whose needs for entertainment include seeing a magnificent show. This type of extravaganza is appealing to those with disposable income, provided they can be convinced of a once-in-a-lifetime experience.

A service designer would instantly recognize all the techniques used by of Cirque De Soleil's for a quality service.

~ ~ ~

Despite the success of Service Design, renown econo-
mists are taking turns on the TED stage to stake out opinions
on whether our services and technology can adequately bring
the Western countries out of their slowing economic growth.

"The Internet revolution is hyped; the industrial world's
greatest productivity occurred during the decades between
the Civil War and just after World War II; and, the golden age
of American growth may be over," Chicago-based economist
Robert Gordon said.

Gordon, though provocative, may not be correct. However, his comments serve to open a meaningful discussion
about ensuring services are well designed to a degree of

quality, that they serve a need, and they generate more revenue than expenses.

The accumulated data makes it evident that since the early 1970s, indeed the U.S. Gross Domestic Product (GDP) has slowed. The GDP is a measure of economic health. There is a correlation between economic well-being and standards of living. The U.S. is not alone in its slow decline, and without improvement, we will impact the next generation's prosperity.

"The trend of deceleration is unequivocal," John Ross said, Senior Fellow at Chong Yang Institute for Financial Studies, Ren Min University of China. "The ten-year growth rate is now only slightly over half."

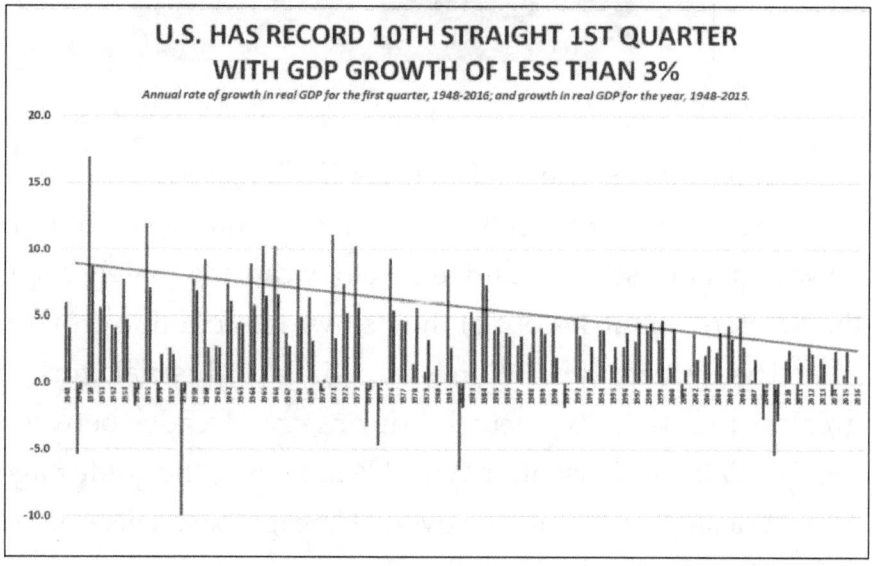

Incidentally (or not), the slowdown coincided with the introduction and growth of information technology and communications. Gordon's comments also highlight the importance of using technology to improve services and better meet the requirements of a quality service mentioned just above.

Gordon's argument is that between 1870 and 1900 the nation's citizens were impressed by the innovations of the day, including rail travel, the growth of catalogue sales by the likes of Sears and Roebuck, and a U.S. Postal Service that could deliver the one-thousand-page catalogue to nearly every household. Yet city streets were not paved, sewage systems and outhouses were synonymous, travel was still an ordeal.

Some thirty-years later, ninety percent of American households had clean running water, electricity, and cars. Another thirty years, skyscrapers filled inner cities, jumbo jets scheduled daily trips with hundreds of passengers across oceans, and man stepped onto the surface of the moon.

"Where is the similar productivity from computers?" Gordon asks. "What have we done with our technology that would amaze someone from one hundred years ago?"

Others believe services are too difficult to quantify for measuring productivity, a view held a former renown economics professor William Baumol. Nonethless, services need to be designed so they are valued.

In 1913, and again one hundred years later in 2013, groups of "Scientific American" readers were asked to list their top-ten all-time inventions. The results showed we are most impressed by innovations that lead to experiences that impact our lives.

The rankings are on perception based of a point in time, Daniel C. Schlenoff said, a journalist-researcher who wrote the article "What Are the 10 Greatest Inventions of Our Time," which appeared in Scientific American.

"In 2013 we might not appreciate the work of Nikola Tesla or Thomas Edison on a daily basis," he said, "as we are accustomed to electricity in all its forms, but we are very impressed by the societal changes caused by the Internet and the World Wide Web (both of which run on alternating-current electricity, by the way). A century from now they might be curious as to what all the fuss was about."

One-hundred years from now, should we expect Scien-tific American readers to list and rank services among the innovations that greatly impacted our lives?

~~~

Frank Sylvester had just gotten into his car when he spotted a Starbucks coffee shop across a four-lane highway. Carefully navigating the intersection, Frank never lost sight of the coffee store's signage. As he got closer, new signs directed him to an enclosed garage within a newly built office tower.

Once inside, Sylvester was forced to choose between a left or a right driveway. With no signs, Sylvester chose the right driveway, which wound up and around a giant pillar up two floors. He drove up until his way was blocked by a ticket gate, with a single sign reading: $5 an hour.

"I couldn't well back down," Sylvester said, animatedly

retelling the story. "I could only hope Starbucks would validate it (the ticket). Otherwise, this little excursion was going cost me a lot more than the cost of a latte."

Starbucks did validate Sylvester's ticket, but from there, his experience headed south. On his way back to his car, nothing looked familiar, he said, even though he was sure he had retraced his steps. When he spotted a security guard, he asked him how to find his car. The guard pointed him to an office, where inside a manager was already dealing with someone else who was lost.

Scientific American	Invention Poll	
1913 Readers Top 10	**Readers Vote 100 Years Later (2013)**
1	Wireless telegraphy	Air Conditioning
2	Aeroplane	Washing Machine
3	X-Ray machine	Traffic Light (Electric)
4	Automobile	Instant Camera
5	Motion pictures	Heart Pacemaker
6	Reinforced concrete	Penicillin production starts
7	Phonograph	Microwave Oven
8	Incandescent electric lamp	Jet Airliner
9	Steam turbine	Smoke Detector
10	Electric car	Cell Phone

It turns out that Sylvester was in the wrong garage The manager pointed him to the opposite wall, across an expansive indoor garage empty of cars, telling Sylvester there were two, five-story garages built back to back. Sylvester just happened to enter the wrong one from Starbucks.

So here we had two massive concrete structures, each with identical color coding corresponding to the floor and nothing distinguishable. There weren't even windows for some orientation.

The gravity of the situation suddenly hit Sylvester hard, he said. He could end up walking up and down, end to end until he stumbled on where he parked. But by then, who knows how long it would take, compounded by having to pay at least $5 extra. But most of all, he confided that he felt a bit of panic from being totally lost, aimlessly wandering.

A half-hour later, Sylvester is still crisscrossing one end to the other, and up and down the stairs. But seeing the Starbucks signs in each staircase gave him an idea to go back to the store and try again. Sure enough, this time walking back everything looked a little different, familiar, and soon Sylvester was at his car. "Let it be known from here to eternity," he told me. "I hope to never be back."

Unlike the lack of signage in the garage, what could otherwise be called user-UNfriendly, Starbucks' managers took great care to ensure drivers could find their store from anywhere in the vicinity: from the intersection a block away, to the parking garage, and from the garage to the store. Yet somehow those who designed the garage, seemed to miss that their mission was to build a parking lot that would be used by drivers.

Unfortunately, missing the point of the user is not an

uncommon phenomenon. For some reason, there is a pervasive mental block preventing those who design and build services and products for users, to consider the user experience. That missing link is particularly noticeable here in the United States where Service Design has yet to catch on. One wonders how the garage would be designed if it served Sylvester's needs along with other drivers.

The lessons from Service Design apply across all services, and will lead answering the cause for why some services fail.

REFERENCES

Jeffrey, T. P. (n.d.). U.S. Has Record 10th Straight 1st Quarter with GDP Growth Less than 3%. (April 28, 2016, 12:27 PM EDT. CNSNews.com.
https://www.cnsnews.com/news/article/us-has-record-10th-straight-1st-quarter-gdp-growth-less-3. Media Research Center.

Schlenoff, D. C. (2013, November 1). What Are the 10 Greatest Inventions of Our Time. Retrieved from https://www.scientificamerican.com/article/inventions-what-are-the-10-greatest-of-our-time. Scientific American.

Triplett, J. E., & Bosworth, B. P. (2000). *Productivity in the Services Sector* (Issue brief). Boston, MA: Brookings Institution. Prepared for: American Economic Association January 7-9, 2000.

2 – SOLVING COMMON CHALLENGES

Members nowadays are hesitant to renew their association memberships, according to recent survey results. The chief reason people join an association is for networking. However, cheaper alternatives are fueling the need for executives to find other approaches to recruit and retain members.

EXECUTIVES RANK INTERNAL CHALLENGES	RANK
Difficulty in communicating VALUE and Benefit	1
Membership too diverse, difficulty meeting needs of different segments	3
Difficulty in proving ROI	4
Difficulty attracting and/or maintaining younger members	6
Lack of a strategy or plan	9
Weak product or service offerings	10
Heidrick & Struggles, Association CEOs Leading Through Change.	

Among executives surveyed, the majority said they could better address membership challenges with a stronger mission or vision plus improved messaging. Recommendations to executives offered by some of the researchers suggest otherwise—that executives abandon the idea of a one-message appeal, or even that their communications would reach its intended target audience.

Instead, Julian Ha, Bill Hudson, and David K. Rehr said in a Heidrick and Struggles report that executives are urged to focus much more on who they serve — and how. They wrote, "The cacophony of voices offering specialized information, services, and advocacy is overwhelming. Executives may want to define their organization's purpose more narrowly. Ultimately, some important activities will be left out of the agenda."

ORGANIZATIONAL CHALLENGES FACING EXECUTIVES (ASAE)
1 Relevant and engaging (attract and retain pipeline of members – including Millennials)
2 Leadership empowerment to set goals, objectives, and priorities (total vision) passionately shared across organization (break down silos)
3 Create and improve non-dues revenue
4 Acquire and implement the "right" technology to benefit an organization's mission
5 Meaningful metrics
Published by ASAE (American Society of Association Executives) 2015

EXECUTIVES RANK INTERNAL CHALLENGES	RANK
Difficulty in communicating VALUE and Benefit	1
Membership too diverse, difficulty meeting needs of different segments	3
Difficulty in proving ROI	4
Difficulty attracting and/or maintaining younger members	6
Lack of a strategy or plan	9
Weak product or service offerings	10
Heidrick & Struggles, Association CEOs Leading Through Change.	

Captured below are highlights from three separate studies with member and executive respondents. The first is a benchmark study intending to determine the health of recruiting and retention. The second study explores motivations behind decisions to join. The third, published by Heidrick and Struggles, examines executives' perspectives on social changes and approaches to managing.

Recruiting, Retention, and Marketing

The benchmark study by Marketing General Inc. (MGI) of Alexandria. Va., is an annual update from prior years. Through the lens of marketing, the firm analyzes the results of recruiting and retention year over year.

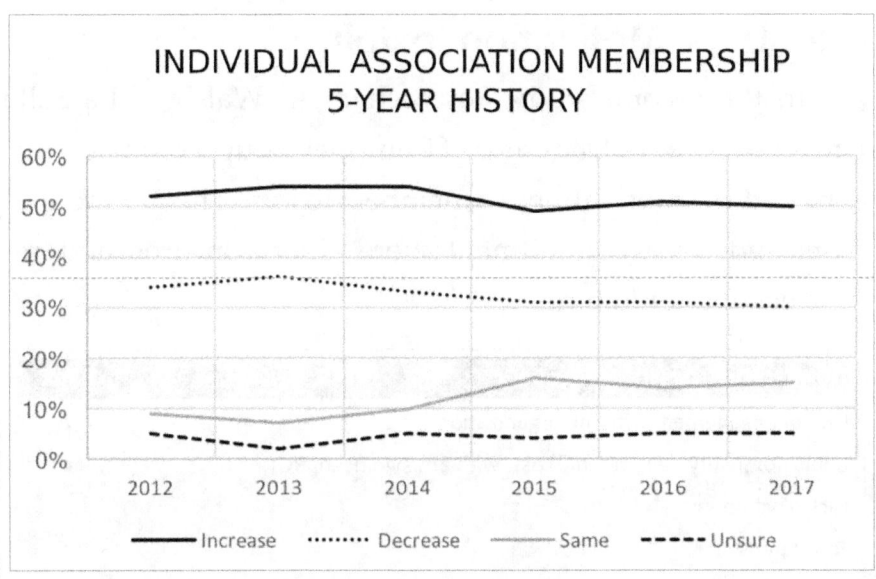

Since 2009, MGI has put forward similar questions to different audience groups, those who self-select to answer. MGI typically garners a 7% response rate from among twenty-thousand who receive the outreach. In its latest 2017 report, nearly half of four hundred forty respondents reported a slight increased-membership growth. A quarter of the respondents reported membership decreases. Researchers found that during the past five years, there has been relatively little change in membership.

However, the average age of members could be concerning. The study found the majority of members are between the ages of 45 and 54. A quarter of the members across the sector are reported to be fifty-four and older. These results seem to underscore the need for a robust pipeline of millennials.

Members' Motivation to Join

In the second study, researchers A. Walsh of La Salle University and K. Daddario of Campbell Soup Company, Inc. explored the motivations of members to join. They found that costs and time commitment were chief concerns and remained so after joining.

Top Reasons for Not Renewing	Rank
Lack of engagement with the organization	2
Could not justify membership costs with any significant ROI	4
Lack of value	7
Too expensive	7
Disappointment with the benefits/services	10
Lack of relevance	12

"The Dynamic Nature of Professional Associations." A. Walsh and K. Daddario
A. Walsh of La Salle University and K. Daddario

The issue of costs went beyond affording annual dues; most said their personal threshold was about one hundred dollars. Many of the respondents told the researchers they had not planned nor expected the added costs of taking advantage of the most desired offerings which included continuing education, credentialing, and meetings—each of which can cost members hundreds of additional dollars.

Consequently, more than a third said they chose not to take part. The authors said they suspected many of the remaining, who did not mention dues and fees, had financial support from employers who paid for their activities.

CONSTRAINTS	PERCENT
Time Constraints	34%
Expensive Dues/Fees	17%
Scheduling of Meeting	13%
Lack of info on other association members	2%
Other	8%
N/A	25%
"The Dynamic Nature of Professional Associations." A. Walsh and K. Daddario	

Their study "The Dynamic Nature of Professional Associations: Factors Shaping Membership Decisions," appeared in the 2015 "Journal of Applied Business and Economics." The criteria they used in selecting study participants were mostly full-time employed MBA students whose ages ranged between 26 and 35. All of them were new members of an association.

Researchers wrote that one of the strongest motivators that swayed a number of members to join was to be part of a well-recognized association. They said, "Professional associations which are well regarded in a particular industry and which offer members opportunities for advancement in the industry, may be well positioned to attract new members."

Executive Share Challenges

The third study focused on how executives perceive and manage change. Among their recommendations, the study authors cautioned executives that "members don't join associations anymore just for networking. They seek a demonstrable return on their investment." They also used executives to reject standard ways of solving challenges. "We find that the traditional role of the association is being challenged, particularly given the tendency of millennials to support specific causes and issues, rather than organizations."

~ ~ ~

Based on the overall findings, one could conclude that a solution to the membership challenges could come about from learning what members value—individually and collectively. If that were possible, a program meeting those needs would have to be sufficiently scaled to be cost effective. These issues will be discussed.

REFERENCES

Ha, J., Hudson, B., & Rehr, D. (2016). Association CEOs: Leading through Change. A survey of more than 500 trade and professional association leaders looks at how they make decisions, approach challenges, and transform their organization in an era of turbulent change. (Rep.). Washington, D.C.: Heidrick & Struggles. By permission.

Rossell, T., Wasserman, I., & Kerr, M. (2017). *2017 Membership Marketing Benchmarking Report* (Rep.). Alexandria, VA: Marketing General, Inc. By permission of MGI.

Walsh, A. M., & Daddario, K. (n.d.). *The Dynamic Nature of Professional Associations: Factors Shaping Membership Decisions* (2015 ed., Vol. Vol. 17(3), pp. 115-125, Publication). Journal of Applied Business and Economics.

3 – DESIGNING SERVICES THAT SUCCEED

Shaping, Improving, Monitoring Services

Service Design techniques are a collection of models and exercises for building services from a user's perspective. As the only practice solely focused on the success of services, executives find the techniques valuable for guiding research and planning, and testing and evaluating a service. When used as intended, the techniques foster membership loyalty, more closely align programs and benefits to member needs, and overall, help sustain an organization for future.

Ideally, an organization's services result in positive experiences for its members and stakeholders. A successful service better defines staff and functional roles, provides clear insights for resource allocation, and serves to unite staff and stakeholders around the organization's mission and purpose.

To achieve a positive experience from a service, the field is organized to encourage teams (who have a mutually shared stake in success), to identify and assemble internal roles, functions, and technology to address each user's actions—hopefully dependent upon a significant level of automation.

The ideal service meets users' expectations. This occurs when an organization's service operations achieve a balance between a boundary—the point at which a user's needs are unmet--and flexibility, in which the service can accommodate variations that inevitably crop up due to the unpredictability of individual preferences.

When a service operates as intended, users are guided along an outcome that is predestined, and mutually satisfies the organization and the user. Therefore, at minimum, a service is user-friendly, intuitive, and unfolds in a way users find logical—without unnecessary distractions (failed website links, for instance). Services that don't meet that threshold are failures. Linda K., a blogger identified as a U.S. Congressional staffer in Washington, D.C., said she avoided or backed out of services that made her feel stupid.

No Two Experiences Are Alike

Services are a big part of our lives, and many of us take them for granted. They are sold out of retail shops, such as dry cleaners; wrapped around products such as the add-on warranties Best Buy offers on electronics. Some services support other services or products. Larger supermarkets, for instance, offer shoppers self-checkout, a cashier line, home delivery, or store pick-up. There are also services dedicated to multiple products or multiple services. Complex office computer hardware and software systems require service expertise to install and maintain.

- **Services materialize as they are used in real time**. They cannot be seen, felt, or tested before purchase. Yet they deliver an intrinsic value to the user.

- **Services are perishable.** Some services are time-sensitive. An empty hotel bed, or an empty airline seat, for instance, is lost revenue that cannot be recovered. For that reason, there are secondary service markets for salvaging potential lost revenue, such as Priceline.com, an online hotel room reseller, and Broadway's TKTS, a surplus Broadway theater ticket reseller.

SERVICES (intangible member benefit programs)	PRODUCTS (tangible member benefits)
• Experienced upon opening or accessing	Completed once shipped
• Capable of successive use for different outcomes, in multiples, in different locations, singularly or by many	N/A
• Monitored (broadly and individually) in real time	N/A
• Quality: Satisfies users' needs, shaped to individual preferences	N/A

Improved with Repeated Use

Capital One bank has for years been nudging its customers to adopt automated banking; but imperfect technology, confusing navigation, and customer distrust got in the way.

Meantime, bank executives explored a variety of measures to shift its customers toward automation. These included requiring tellers to redirect and instruct customers, offer financial incentives, and redesigning branches with automated stations equipped with iPads.

Yet it is unclear how bank executives have been measuring success. While it is obvious more customers have turned to automation for deposits, transfers, and online payments, the result is fewer physical branches, less personnel, and fewer opportunities to cross sell other financial products and services. It is also uncertain which factors motivated customers to use automation. Was it improved navigation, convenience, trust, or something else?

No doubt consumer tastes have changed to match the ever-rapid pace of technology in our lives. Capital One executives said recently that they have incorporated Service Design techniques to help evolve their services from here on.

Chapter II
Creating Positive Experiences

"All experiences impact on one's future, for better or worse."

—John Dewey

4 – SEEKING THE LODESTONE

Walt Disney Company's focus never veers from making people happy. Its entire operation focuses on making people happy—this is their *service concept* from the design of its rides to the conduct of its personnel to the vibes received from ubiquitous festive themes—and just about everything else.

A good friend's daughter left her teddy bear at a Disney resort which can easily manifest into a catastrophe for a four-year-old. But Disney has toy rescue operators for which "hosts" and "characters" fan out in rapid response. The next morning, the young girl found her teddy bear on the family's doorstep, special delivery. Inside, her teddy bear was comfortably nestled in padding, and any past heartache was gone. All that was left was a positive experience from the resort.

In the Disney example, a cynic might interpret the service concept as clever branding. But a service concept is much more—it drives the branding. The service concept is the purpose for the organization's existence, the compass heading for goal setting and objectives. Everything else therefore, including behind-the-scenes, must align.

Among associations, the service concept is the why and wherefore that motivates members to join and engage. The service concept, in other words, is the mutual affinity, the must-be-preserved between individuals and the organization. Service concepts are the pivotal factor for evaluating ideas for new member services and programs.

The service concept is the why and wherefore that motivates members to join and engage. It is also the attraction for dedicated employees and the glue that binds staff together toward a common mission and purpose.

Service concepts must be carefully considered and purposefully designed to meet the following:

- Encompass—or help to define—the organization's purpose;
- Have meaning, be easily understood;
- Be appropriate throughout organization;
- Have a decent chance of lasting.

Service concepts are the measure to be used for evaluating new ideas for member services and programs.

A company that displays its service concept at every opportunity is Southwest Airlines. As the company describes its service concept on their website: "Southwest has been in LUV with our Customers from the very beginning. We began service to San Antonio and Houston from Love Field in Dallas. As our company and customers grew, our LUV grew too with the prettiest flight attendants serving 'Love Bites' and tickets issued from our 'Love Machines.' Our LUV has spread from coast to coast and border to border." Even the company's stock ticker symbol is LUV.

Service Evaluation Tool

New program ideas often come about from interacting with members and discovering their needs. Most ideas are worth evaluating if only to determine whether they will better serve the organization.

SERVICE EVALUATION TEMPLATE

(SERVICE CONCEPT)

OBJECTIVE
Describe what you are attempting to accomplish—goal, solve, correct.

TARGET NEEDS
Describe need service will fulfill.

AVAILABLE RESOURCES
ID governance, staff, partners, volunteers, technology, costs and funding.

DRIVER(S)
What is driving the need?

TARGET AUDIENCE
Who will be served directly? (Segment and sub-segments)

CONSTRAINTS
Parameters that define, restrict, or contain outcome.

RISKS
Identify risks of failure.

TRENDS
Trends to piggyback?

INTERNAL BARRIERS
Internal obstacles?

DECIDE TO TAKE NEXT STEPS – TO SERVICE BLUEPRINT?   Go ___   No ___

Still, it is so much easier to dismiss a new idea than

explore its merit. Many organizations are risk-adverse and executives simply find it easier to say "no" to avoid disruption. That thinking, however, results in missed opportunities. Quickly evaluating new ideas helps avoid spending resources on worthless pursuits—and helps to select the ones with greater chance of proving worthwhile to both the organization and members.

Program ideas for associations, meantime, have to strike a balance between the organization's needs and resources, and members' desires—and most of all, further the organization's service concept. Some find a service evaluation tool helpful. The tool brings together the service concept, the needs of the organization and its members, and helps decision-makers identify potential risks for going forward with a new service.

The service evaluation tool works particularly well in team environments for sharing decision ownership. The tool will illuminate considerations, and possibly later serve as a roadmap to its implementation. Someone might ask a rider getting out of an Uber car, "How was your ride?" Their question refers to the service system. They are most likely interested in knowing about traffic conditions, whether the driver was able to navigate to your destination, and any other incidents that occurred along the way. A horrible experience, meantime, will not prevent someone from using Uber again.

A service system refers to the combination of technology, process, and people for creating a user experience. The service system uses these resources to fulfill users' needs.

A service operation is made up of a provider's

functions—departments such as accounting, IT, membership, marketing, events, member programing, and so forth. Each department has ownership of a portion of the operation, and together they function to create a reliable, repeatable service.

A McDonald's restaurant is a perfect example. Servers take orders, charge customers, and complete as much of the order as they can. Sometimes the customer requests a special order, and the server draws upon the larger team to make it happen. Each of the stores are identical with technology, people roles, and process, all working to deliver a service. The stores, if you will, are the human interface helping the experience unfold.

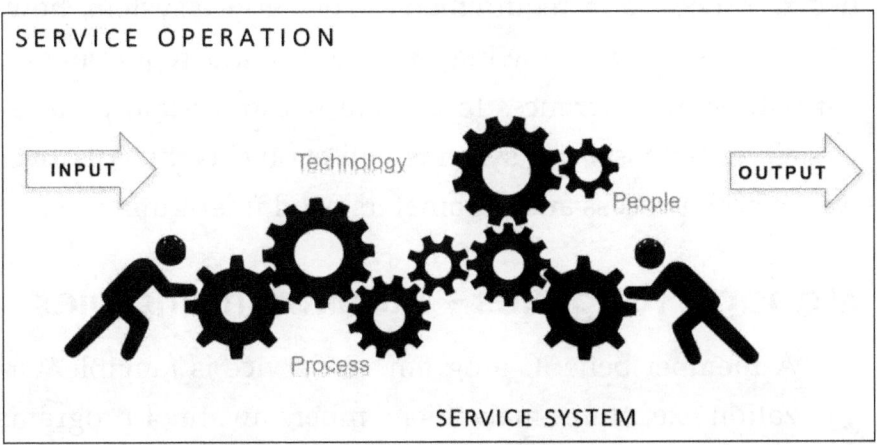

The McDonald's service system allows the company to satisfy millions of customers by requiring its stores to adhere to standards and requirements. If we could see the service operation, it would be organized by food purchasing and packaging, store design, food preparation equipment, staffing, and training. The company trains its staff in process and procedures. The grill staff, for example, follows explicit manuals. Failure at the store level is when people fail to adhere to the corporate standards.

Most service operations are out of sight from the users. Airbnb's service operations are revealed, somewhat, through the options it offers owners, including whether Airbnb should collect municipal taxes, charge for cleaning services, require signed rental contracts, and collect and refund security deposits—with each function linked to a separate corporate department.

No matter, the service operation will ultimately succeed in delivering reliable and repeatable services, since they are tied to process and requirements. The service system, however, succeeds by following the process and requirements, yet with some tolerances to deviate within certain parameters. Over time, service systems will evolve as they discover where both process and parameters need finer tuning.

Manage Tangibles – Monitor Intangibles

A member benefit, program, or service is tangible. Organization executives make its members aware of programs with hopes they choose to participate.

Their choice may be influenced by a tangible outcome such as a certification or a recertification credit. The program, the activities, the credits, and certification are all considered tangibles. Tangibles are managed as service operations for consistency. Tangibles also generate user experiences. A positive experience draws in more users. Experiences are intangible.

TANGIBLES	INTANGIBLES			
PROGRAMS	Networking	Innovations & Developments	Education & Training	Awards & Recognition
Events	◆	◆	◆	◆
SIGS, Committees	◆	◆		◆
Industry Research		◆		
Certification	◆		◆	◆
Sponsorships	◆			◆
Publishing: (Newsletters, magazines, peer-reviewed journals)		◆	◆	◆

By monitoring intangibles, managers gain greater degrees of control over the experience.

5 – BUILDING A FAN BASE

For those who count on satisfaction surveys to measure performance, they are a waste, says a renowned business strategist. "Glowing customer satisfaction surveys don't correlate tightly with profits or growth," Fred Reichheld said. "Most senior executives, board members, and investors don't take them very seriously."

Reichheld, known for the Net Promoter Score, stumbled on the idea for his famous business model while consulting for Enterprise Rent-A-Car. Executives there were singularly focused on discovering its customers' positive experiences—deconstructing them for lessons to share across the company's stores.

The way this worked was, Enterprise would survey customers when they returned the cars asking them if they would recommend Enterprise to others. Managers would then sort through the responses looking for those who said they would. All the others were thrown away.

As Enterprise vaulted to the top of the rental market, Reichheld wanted to see whether there was a strong correlation between its market growth and the company's approach to positive experiences. After research studies and further testing, Reichheld conceived the Net Promoter Score, or NPS.

Net Promoter Score (NPS)

The Net Promoter Score differs from a satisfaction survey in that NPS reflects loyalty while satisfaction surveys reflect someone's attitude at the time of completing a service. Reichheld's NPS uses a similar approach to that of Enterprise, asking respondents whether they would recommend the service to others. Respondents are asked to choose one of ten answer choices—from 1, the lowest, to 10 the highest.

A Net Promoter Score reflects the loyalty of members to the organization, program, or service. Scores are between one and one-hundred, with an average score topping out at about 20, which consequently correlates to the 80/20 rule. That rule, also known as the Pareto principle, suggests 80% of income originates with just 20% of a customer base.

How to Score

Using the Net Promoter Score is quite straightforward. Responses, one through 10, are sorted into three categories: Promoters, Passives, and Detractors. The score is calculated by totaling the categories and subtracting.

Net Promoter Score Question

How likely is it that you would recommend this company to a friend or colleague?

(1) (2) (3) (4) (5) (6) (7) (8) (9) (10)

NOT LIKELY   LIKELY

Net Promoter Score Question

- Add Totals
  - Add totals for 9s and 10s (x) "Promoters"
  - Add totals 7s and 8s (y) "Passives"
  - Add totals 0-to-6s (z) "Detractors"
- Normalize totals—converting the numbers into percentages (x/100=%, y/100=%, z/100=%).
  - Then subtract Promoters (x) from Detractors (z).
  - Convert result back to a positive integer.
  - Finally, weight the result using the total percentage of Detractors:
    - If "Passives" exceeds fifty percent of the total responses, add five points.

Categories in Detail

- **Promoters (9s and 10s):** Members (customers) are intensely loyal and are willing to put their reputations on the line to recommend the service to others. These are the most highly valued members and can be counted on to discuss the service with others and to promote its benefits.
- **Passives (7s and 8s):** They are somewhat satisfied, but uncertain whether to repeat their experience. These members could be tempted away by competing offers that satisfy the same need. Their lack of enthusiasm will prevent them from supporting your service(s), or talking them up with others. However, these members are not likely to be corrosive by spreading negativity about the organization.
- **Detractors (0 to 6s):** They are the least likely to repeat their

experience and are likely to take advantage of related, follow-on offerings or be tempted by discounts. These are fairly negative members overall, whose negativity could spill out beyond one-time experiences causing the organization harm.

NPS Strategies

Firstly, organizations should direct key resources to promoters, since they are the primary audience—the sustainers. Promoters help new ideas take hold, both by their participation and by bringing others along. Investments in promoters are the most likely to result in a return on investment. Ideally, organizations are nurturing their promoter personas, staying current with their audiences' needs and interests—and fulfilling them.

Secondly, there are immense benefits to matching uncovered real-life individuals who match fictitious personas. If the organization does not yet use personas, they should begin developing ones for each of the three NPS categories. Over time—using real individuals to validate and strengthen the personas—to create and improve member benefits and programs.

Thirdly, some will branch out beyond promoters and reach to passives for converting some of their numbers into promoters. This approach requires great care to ensure passives are continually satisfied. Yet if successful, some passives will be receptive to ever increasing involvement, closer ties, and conversions to promoters.

For Enterprise Rent-A-Car, however, all of these strategies

were moot. The company had no interest in their individual customers. Their aim was to identify a successful experience and deconstruct it so they could replicate it elsewhere—anywhere among seventy-two thousand Enterprise locations.

Uber Can't Fail

I am not a frequent Uber user by any measure, yet I am in awe of aspects of the service. For one, it operates seamlessly—anywhere. A U.S.-based reporter for the Washington Post recently wrote about his surprise upon finding the service was as reliable in Moscow as in D.C. As a service operation, it meets the hallmarks of quality. The service is predictable and reliable for riders, and replicable and scalable for organizations.

I bet most riders take for granted that when the Uber app is used to request a ride, the system's algorithms find and alert nearby drivers who choose whether to accept a fare.

Birth of Uber

The idea for Uber came from Garrett Camp, a Canadian who built a successful web business in graduate school while attending the University of Calgary. He and Travis Kalanick, a computer engineer who dropped out of UCLA after his own success launching a web-based business, thought the public would benefit from a one-click app that would call a cab.

Those two brought in Oscar Salazar Gaitan, a Mexican telecom and engineering graduate, to design the architecture of on-demand world-wide transportation, and Conrad Whelan, a Computer Systems Engineer graduate from Holland who specialized in equations of electromagnetic physics for device design. By 2009, they had built a prototype.
Source:
www.businessinsider.com/ubers-history

choose whether to accept a fare.

Once accepted, the application synchs riders and drivers.

Then the driver's photo, name, car model and color, license plate, and location appear in the app. Through the algorithms, drivers and riders are able to locate each other, even in the middle of a crowded intersection. That sequence of events is carefully orchestrated through Uber's service operation.

Additionally, riders can expect courteous drivers in a clean odorless car. Riders can also expect drivers to stay faithful to the GPS directions that are proprietary to Uber, created by Google Maps. The entire activity unfolds exactly as the company intended: satisfying riders' and drivers' needs with a satisfying experience.

The challenge was to design a service that could accomplish consistent one-way rides initiated by riders with one tap on an application. Automation, coupled with unknown vehicles, random drivers, and millions of passengers throughout areas of the world, would need to marry up seamlessly to deliver consistent and reliable favorable experiences.

Relying on automation, designers had to balance between flexibility and outright service failure. Put another way—for the system to be repeatable and function predictably, it had to accommodate deviations that would undoubtedly occur, to withstand unpredictable circumstances. This was solved by designing the system in functional components. Whelan, a device designer, would have likely relied on a Service Design Blueprint to map out each function and its interaction generated by the rider. With a blueprint, the group would have realized that automation around procedures would have to remain inflexible, or static. That was the only way to reliably scale the service across the globe. To allow for flexibility, the model allows the drivers to decide.

| 2 | WHAT YOUR RIDERS SAID |

5.0 ★

DRIVER RATING
Nice work, your driver rating last week was above average.

RIDER FEEDBACK
You received **33** five-star reviews out of 34 rated trips in the past two weeks. We wanted to share what some of these riders had to say.

"Best ride I've had on Uber! "

"Great drive!"

Giving drivers decision-making to accommodate riders is governed, in a way, by how drivers are compensated for a completed journey. Anything that a driver agrees to outside of a journey is unpaid. It is up to drivers to decide whether to wait for riders, for instance, or to veer off from the GPS proscribed route, or just anything else.

The design for Uber was developed into a prototype to

test where possible failures could occur. The designers then put in place measures to prevent unintended conse-quences, particularly important given that the entire operation was designed to be automated. It is also through testing that they were able to craft driver standards needed to maintain a consistent, reliable experience.

A service operation on the other hand, governs the service with standards and requirements—and either provides resources directly for the service system, or provides the guidance for obtaining the resources. Airbnb, an online short-term housing rental service, is a company that might be familiar to some. Renters use the service to find properties worldwide. Property owners post their properties on Airbnb for perspective renters to find. Its operation is part advertiser and part broker, wholesaler. They also manage the financial transactions and some of the legal aspects

Airbnb's technology pulls all the parts together, yet the company

The Knowledge

The famed London taxi, also known as cabbies, black cabs and hackney carriages, are considered the most heavily regulated inner-city ride service.

Most Londoners are aware of the rigorous standards required for vehicle maintenance. But it is the incredibly strict requirements for drivers, known as The Knowledge," which attracts worldwide interest.

"It has been called the hardest test, of any kind, in the world. Its rigors have been likened to those required to earn a degree in law or medicine. It is without question a unique intellectual, psychological, and physical ordeal, demanding unnumbered thousands of hours of immersive study" to memorize the entirety of London. One must demonstrate that mastery through a progressively more difficult sequence of oral examinations—a process which, on average, takes four years to complete."

Matt McCabe, 33, spent three years studying London's roads and landmarks, and how to navigate between them. "In the process, he had logged more than fifty thousand miles on motorbike and on foot, the equivalent of two circumnavigations of the Earth, nearly all within inner London's dozen boroughs and the City of London's financial district. He was studying to be a London taxi driver, devoting himself full-time to the challenge."

Source: The New York Times Style Magazine. (Rosen)

is barely part of the renter's perceived experience. Renters attach their experiences to the owners' properties. If that experience is unpleasant, Airbnb is mostly insulated. Its brokerage-style business model transfers the responsibility for meeting renters' expectations and delivering a positive experience on the owners. Despite all its testing and superb functionality, Uber is continually defending what others say is an unfair competitive advantage. The company's surge, or "dynamic" pricing, is when fares rise exorbitantly during high demand. This can occur when riders have few if any other options, occurring due to traffic tie-ups or severe weather. There have been reports that surge pricing has been in effect during disaster evacuations.

More common is Uber's disruption to traditional transportation systems. In New York and London, for instance, taxi services are heavily regulated and require owners and drivers to be licensed. Licenses in New York City cost $1.3 million for what is called a medallion. Uber drivers, though, do not yet have to conform.

In London, the municipalities governing the city have refused to license Ubers (see inset above, "The Knowledge"). In Washington, D.C., Uber has the potential to further cripple its cash-strapped Metro rail and bus service. Metro, once hailed as a panacea to the commuter woes of one of the most traffic-congested cities in the U.S., already relies on a one hundred fifty million-dollar infusion from the federal government. Ridership has dropped since a short system-closing forced riders to find other transportation. Apparently sufficient numbers of commuters preferred Uber car pools to the crowded Metro, and many have not returned. This has led to increased fares and less service, Metro's General Manager Paul Wiedefeld said.

REFERENCES

McAlone, A. H. (2016, August 01). The story of how Travis Kalanick built Uber into the most feared and valuable startup in the world. Retrieved February 15, 2018, from http://www.businessinsider.com/ubers-history. Business Insider.

Rogers, F. F. (2014, July 31). Motivating Through Metrics. Retrieved February 15, 2018, from https://hbr.org/2005/09/motivating-through-metrics. Harvard Business Review.

Rood, S. (2016, September 26). How D.C. Metro Can Bring Riders Back. Retrieved February 15, 2018, from https://nextcity.org/daily/entry/dc-metro-ridership-bring-passengers-back. Next City.

Rosen, J. (2014, November 10). The Knowledge, London's Legendary Taxi-Driver Test, Puts Up a Fight in the Age of GPS. Retrieved February 15, 2018, from https://www.nytimes.com/2014/11/10/t-magazine/lon-don-taxi-test-knowledge.html.

6 – SATISFY USER NEEDS

Audience Needs

Laszlo Büch, a Holocaust survivor from the former Czechoslovakia, made his way to New York City after World War II. Ten years later, he had anglicized his name to Leslie Burk, and joined Kensington, Connecticut-based Sherri Cup Company, a struggling startup looking to break into the New York City coffee cup market.

Burk, a salesman for Sherri, came upon an idea to design a cup without a handle that could carry hot liquids; a product we now take for granted. Burk's idea solved a need on behalf of the on-the-go coffee drinker.

Burk also wanted a design that would-be buyers, the diner owners, would find irresistible—a Greek-themed cup with a welcoming hospitality message. The finished product was a four-inch high cup with a blue solid background, white Greek meander top and bottom, and a white shield on opposite sides separated by two amphorae. Inside each shield are images of three cups of coffee with abundant trails of steam, and the words "We Are Happy to Serve You," appearing to materialize in the piping hot steam. Yes, all that on a hand-held paper cup.

All through the 1990s the "Head," as it became known, sold more than four billion cups a year, trailing off until it was no longer manufactured in 2010, the year Burk died at age 87. Over the years, the cup's appeal has shifted from its functionality to its design, an iconic image representing New  York City. Today the cup is a common theater, movie, and television prop to convey an earlier, grittier time. The Anthora cup was recently spilled in the recently released acclaimed Netflix show *Mind-Hunter,* and George Clooney held on to one as Michael Clayton did in the eponymous movie also trending now on Netflix.

"It was for decades the most enduring piece of ephemera in New York City, and is still among the most recognizable," New York Times reporter (Fox) wrote in Burk's obituary.

It remains known as the Anthora cup because of Burk's difficulty pronouncing "th" from his earlier years growing up in Europe before he spoke English. Burk served as Sherri's chief marketer and salesman until retirement.

The Anthora vignette demonstrates the importance of recognizing the market. Burk discovered he needed to satisfy the end users, coffee drinkers, not his direct buyers, the Greek diner proprietors. His buyers may never have perceived the poor design of the cup, and thus were unable to satisfy their own customers. His contribution was widespread, helping coffee shop owners around New York City satisfy millions of customers with a positive experience.

Uncover User Needs with Personas

Personas slice a portion of the market for targeting — grouping like-minded characteristics into manageable segments. Some confuse a persona with a real person. But they are merely fictional representations of groups with a commonality. These groupings could be demographic (age range, gender, job titles, and responsibilities); lifestyle (member benefit usage, preferences, goals, and ambitions); geographic location; an interest (IT savvy, early technology adopters); or any other attribute that would make sense for identifying target group.

Crafting a persona involves collecting sufficient data to identify common needs, behavior, and motivations.

Validate Persona - attributes, goals, communicate

	The Millennial (Calvin)	The Professional (Val)	The Promoter (Gail)
	Seek out goals – encourage participation, i.e. lead responsibilities, tap for peer outreach ideas.	Training, continuing education, certification, mentee. Publications	Events, meetings, board involvement, mentor. Publications
	What's in it for Me?	Seeks professional advancement – credentials	Networker, Information Sharing. Stays Current.

Millennials
Reach: Informal networking – peer-based (through employer?)

Professional (members)
Reach: Track professional development toward goals – assessments, training, certifications. (Consider automating through Learning Management System)

Promoters
Reach: Keep involved through volunteer leadership, for agenda–setting policy

Seek Testimonials

There are no limits to the number of personas one can create per program or service. But more than, say, three or four will introduce levels of complexity that will eventually scuttle the program. Too many personas tend to be re-source-heavy, and offer few opportunities to recover costs.

Personas evolve over time as group characteristics become better known—leading to more valuable insights. Executives can use personas to gain feedback from users about programs and services, including when and how programs become known, which needs are satisfied, and incentives that drive motivation. Personas are also useful for identifying preferred communications.

Others find personas useful for placing products. Ruth Staltz began working for a trend-setting product line we will call Gizmo which produces products of the same name—Gizmos. The product is a fad, and Gizmos are riding the wave of popularity. As an observer, I have yet to figure out whether its success is due to inspiration, perseverance, well-placed connections, or sheer dumb luck. Regardless, Staltz's assignment was to chase the competition by finding retailers carrying similar products. From there, it was someone else's responsibility on staff, from sales, to contact the retailer and get a placement on store shelves.

To my thinking, this was upside down. The company's strategy was likely churning Staltz's time with meager results. Instead, personas would serve the company well. By developing personas to represent its ideal audience and target markets—categorized by how the Gizmo would be used—Staltz' efforts would prove far more effective. The sales staff would have personas to convince retailers that by carrying Gizmo's they were serving their customer needs. Instead, Gizmo sales staff just had the "how about me, too" strategy, and a built-in hurdle of competition for shelf-space with a near identical product.

Personas are ideal for dissecting larger markets and uncovering common needs. Besides, the activity and results allow you to understand ideal targets in ways that are empowering. These include solving challenges that require stakeholder input and uncovering motivations, brainstorming ways to serve personas' needs, and for testing and validating assumptions.

Personas evolve over time as group characteristics become better known—leading to more valuable insights. Executives can use personas to gain feedback from users about programs and services, including when and how programs become known, which needs are satisfied, and incentives that drive motivation. Personas are also useful for identifying preferred communications.

Others find personas useful for placing products. Ruth Staltz began working for a trend-setting product line, we will call Gizmo, which produces products of the same name—Gizmos. The product is a fad, and Gizmos are riding the wave of popularity. As an observer, I have yet to figure out whether its success is due to inspiration, perseverance, well-placed connections, or sheer dumb luck. Regardless, Staltz's assignment was to chase the competition by finding retailers carrying similar products. From there, it was someone else's responsibility on staff, from sales, to contact the retailer and get a placement on store shelves.

To my thinking, this was upside down. The company's strategy was likely churning Staltz's time with meager results. Instead, personas would serve the company well. By developing personas to represent its ideal audience and target markets—categorized by how the Gizmo would be used—Staltz' efforts would prove far more effective. The sales staff would have personas to convince retailers that by carrying Gizmo's they were serving their customer needs. Instead, Gizmo sales staff just had the "how about me, too" strategy, and a built-in hurdle of competition for shelf-space with a near identical product.

Personas are ideal for dissecting larger markets and uncovering common needs. Besides, the activity and results allow you to understand ideal targets in ways that are empowering. These include solving challenges that require stakeholder input and uncovering motivations, brainstorming ways to serve personas' needs, and for testing and validating assumptions.

PERSONA TEMPLATE

Name   Name the Persona (i.e. "The Millennials")

Description   Describe the Target; Value in Joining, Renewing

Quote   "I could be interested if I knew who I would be networking with . . "
"What are the ways I could become involved; what value do I get?"

Demographics
- Age Range
- Job Title
- Category:

Attitudes   Categorized by:
- A point of view;
- Typical NPS score;
- Descriptions to quickly identify this persona

Goals
- Motivations

Behavior
- Channel preference?
- Trend-maker/follower?
- Drawn by cost?
- Seeking personal benefit?
- Identifiable need?

The Mission? • Based on data mission to complete above – or any other useful data

REPRESENTATIVE PHOTOGRAPH

In the Spirit of Personas

I can think of no better example of a company other than Spirit Airlines whose business is reliant upon personas. The company's ideal customer is the head of a household who works all year for a family vacation whose need is travel to and from a destination. Moreover, this market's attitude reflects the view that travel is a necessary inconvenience.

Spirit is loosely modeled on Ryan Air's no-frills shuttle that transports passengers between European cities for roughly forty dollars a trip. Ryan Air, whose concept is nothing more than a flying bus, solves the needs of several personas: First, transporting a massive international student market that needs fast, inexpensive travel between cities. Second, business access to the newly formed "single market," allowing business travelers to line up meetings throughout a single day, and arrive back at home that evening. And third, as a last-minute option for nationals to spend a weekend visiting friends and family.

Each of these needs arose from the formation of the European Union. Prior to this, despite the proximity between countries, with many of its residents living on or near each other's borders, most countries made great efforts to see that nationals did not cross over for jobs. The EU helped in that regard by requiring member countries to do away with restrictive travel visa requirements.

The needs of Spirit's market, however, could not be more different. Unlike short hops in Europe, passengers on Spirit spend hours, if not an entire day, getting from point to point, due to vast distances between cities in the United States. All the while, its ideal market seems just fine enduring whatever it takes to reach the other end, because passengers are feeling enormously satisfied that they just saved a few bucks.

Schlepping large bags—that's an extra cost on Spirit. A drink or snack—an extra cost. Reclining seats—non-existent on Spirit. Anyone accustomed to the services offered on other airlines will be horrified by the continual failure to meet expectations. These are travelers Spirit was not targeting, and who were drawn in by the lure of lower base fares.

Jennifer Lawson, a fourteen-year-old, returning from camp in Houston, Texas, was traveling Spirit to the East Coast about two thousand miles or halfway across the country. Prior to boarding, Jennifer laid out the rest of her cash at the ticket counter to cover the costs of a bag fee, plus ten dollars to print the boarding pass.

During the flight, Jennifer became extremely thirsty and asked an attendant for water. The stewardess put out her hand for seven dollars. Jennifer told the attendant she had already spent the rest her money at the counter to get on the plane, to which the attendant said, "There are no exceptions," and she walked away.

Jennifer got out of her seat and followed the attendant down the aisle protesting. She did not need a whole bottle, she told the attendant, just a few sips. So, the attendant held open the bathroom door and offered her the bathroom sink, which was labeled "non-potable."

A Google search of "Spirit Airlines" brings up many hits devoted to agitated travelers sharing stories and venting about their negative experiences. The U.S. Department of Transportation reported in 2016 that nearly twelve out of every one-hundred thousand passengers file complaints with the U.S. government against Spirit Airlines, more than seven times more any other airline. A blogger, whose website defends the airline's practices, wrote: "Spirit guarantees customers will arrive at their destination, even if it's three days later."

Yet by financial measures, Spirit Airlines is a winner in a competitive industry in which most airlines, if they meet profitability, do so by the slimmest of margins. Moreover, Spirit's stock shares have doubled since their offering in 2008—riding through the stormy Great Recession, emerging as the industry leader.

Spirit's "Bare Fare" explanation is hard to miss when booking online. In large, clear, bold, colorful lettering—animated with short, almost edgy videos—travelers are educated in the "Spirit way" of packing a bag. Central to the message of low cost is that anything adding weight to the plane increases the cost of fuel, a fee which Spirit needs to pass on to its passengers.

So how does Spirit achieve positive balance statements while at the same time accumulating unprecedented dissatisfaction? The airline has mastered its ideal target using a persona, and regardless of its detractors, there are plenty of fans willingly to suck it up for the benefit of low-cost flying.

REFERENCES

Airline On-Time Statistics. (2017, June 14). Retrieved February 15, 2018, from https://www.bts.gov/newsroom/airline-consumer-complaints-previous-year-march-2017. Bureau of Transportation Statistics.

Fox, M. (2010, April 29). Leslie Buck, Designer of Iconic Coffee Cup Dies at 87. Retrieved February 15, 2018, from http://www.nytimes.com/2010/04/30/nyregion/30buck.html. The New York Times.

Shevlin, R. (2015, November 23). The Future of Venmo. Retrieved February 15, 2018, from https://thefinancialbrand.com/55401/the-future-of-venmo/. The Financial Brand.

Chapter III
Motivating Users

"The most effective way to stir emotions is through language and images, well-crafted to work simultaneously."

—Hansjörg Hohr, professor at the
Department of Educational Research,
UiO Department of Education, Norway, Oslo

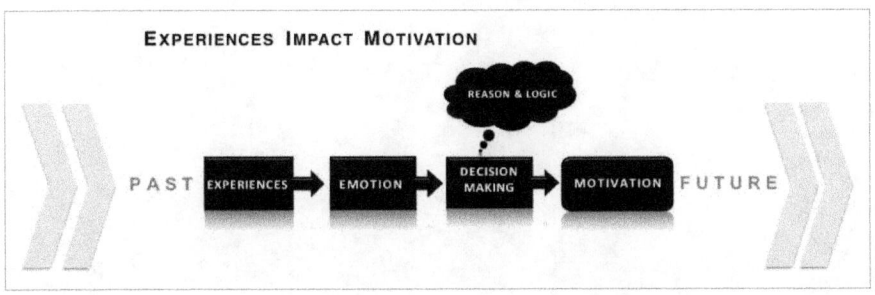

7 – THE PATH TO MOTIVATION

Experiences are inseparable from emotions, according to a noted expert in aesthetic experiences. Emotions occur from a range of experiences, Professor Hansjörg Hohr said, a professor at the Department of Educational Research, UiO Department of Education, Norway, Oslo. He includes among those experiences hearing stories, observing art-work, and interacting with certain objects.

Emotions result in motivation, Hohr wrote in "The Concept of Experience by John Dewey Revisited," an abstract reflecting the work of aesthetic emotions founder John Dewey.

"When we are young, it doesn't take much to stimulate our emotions," he said. "But as we get older, motivations become more complex. We tend to introduce reason and logic. The heart and head possibly come in conflict with each other."

~ ~ ~

Spurring motivation is a significant challenge which the Government Employees Insurance Company, or Geico, has tackled with great success. The company relies on a direct-to-consumer sales model, an advantage that helps reduce costs so it can theoretically charge policy holders less. The flip side is having to influence or motivate consumers to take the steps of signing up online or calling a company-salaried representative. Even in the best circumstances, selling insurance policies is difficult. Consumers only think about insurance coverage when making a claim, according to consumer research.

To overcome these obstacles, Geico has piled staggering amounts of money into advertising, more than $1 billion a year, to target audiences with messages that might be considered as either incredibly subtle, or too over the top.

The firm responsible for Geico's messaging, The

Does Geico's Gecko Sell Insurance?

For nearly 60 years, Geico was an obscure niche marketer of automobile insurance. The company's growth strategy depended almost exclusively on direct mail targeting a select group with exceptional driving records.

When the company launched in 1936, its target audience was strictly federal government employees, with a greater focus on the top tiers of non-commissioned officer military ranks. In the U.S. Army and U.S. Air Force, this group is ranked from Chief Master Sergeant on down. At the end of its first year, the company had 3,700 policyholders.

Little changed over the decades until 1994, when the company decided to expand its client base and hired The Martin Agency, an IPG shop in Richmond, Virginia, to produce national TV, radio, and print ads, branching out from just direct mail efforts. In 1996 billionaire investor Warren Buffett, bought the company as a wholly owned subsidiary of Berkshire Hathaway. When Buffett met Geico's Marketing Director, Ted Ward, "He told us to keep doing what we were doing, just do it faster."

From 1996 on, ad spending nearly doubled each year through to 2000. Between 2004 and 2006, Geico had increased its ad spending by 75%, according to Ad Age. Its media buy alone, was $500 million, twice what its nearest competitor spent. If I could have spent $2 billion placing advertising, I would have, Buffett is reported saying.

In 2007, J.D. Power ranked Geico fourth among all auto insurance companies in the U.S., and pronounced the company as number one in customer acquisition, at 5.8%.

By 2012, the company's advertising budget never dipped below $1 billion a year. Five years later, Geico reported spending $1.5 billion for advertising. (http://adage.com/article/news/geico-s-big-spending-pays-study/118844/).

Martin Agency based in Richmond Virginia, is credited with the birth of talking pigs, recognizable cavemen characters, and a little green cartoon lizard—and of course, the enduring, alliterative tagline, "Fifteen minutes can save you fifteen percent or more."

Mike Boyd, a former Vice President and Managing Supervisor at The Martin Agency, acknowledged the challenge of selling insurance through advertising. "You tend to want to keep the message simple," he offered, adding, "We wanted to show people that Geico is different."

Cheering on Geico's advertising is no less than renown investor Warren Buffett, who as chairman and CEO of Geico's parent, Berkshire Hathaway, began investing in the company at age 21. The multibillionaire, known in part for his modest lifestyle, took ownership of the company when it was in near collapse, and helped its rescue by large investments in advertising.

J.D. Power, a consumer auto ranking company, lists Geico as the second largest U.S. auto insurer behind State Farm, and continuing to outpace its nearest rivals. Writing to shareholders recently, Buffett predicted: "On August 30, 2030—my 100th birthday—I plan to announce that GEICO has taken over the top spot. Mark your calendar."

Date	Message	Campaign	Conveyed
1999	Correct pronunciation of the name – GEICO.	Introducing the gecko character.	*"I am a gecko, not to be confused with GEICO."*
1999-Current	Gecko mascot instantly recognizable for delivering message.	Chris the GEICO Gecko.	
2004	Dispel any notion of difficulty getting online and signing up.	"So Easy a Caveman Could Do It."	*The characters are affluent, educated, and cultured. The humor revolves around the relative normality of the cavemen, and their reactions to their stereotype—and attempt to defend themselves.*
2008	Saving money is possible by switching to GEICO.	"The Money You Could Be Saving"	*Two paper-banded stacks of U.S. bills—with a pair of big, googly eyes, stares at people (in an unsettling way), set to "Somebody's Watching Me," a remix of a Rockwell/Michael Jackson song,*
2009-2012	By now the message should be obvious that you could save money switching to GEICO (Rhetorical Questions Campaign).	"Could Switching to GEICO Really Save You 15% Or More On Car Insurance?"	*Did the little piggy cry 'wee wee wee' all the way home?? -- Maxwell the pig.*

In addition to outspending its rivals on advertising for a larger market share, Geico's direct-to-consumer model could not be better timed given the emerging market of millennials. Ethnologists and demographers tell us those born between 1982 and 1996 prefer online interaction over dealing directly with sales agents, and are entirely comfortable with experiences that begin and end through the internet. The millennials, who are today between ages 20 and 35 years old, already account for $600 billion a year spent on consumer goods, according to *Adweek*. And by 2030—the year Buffett predicts Geico will de-thrown State Farm for the top spot in auto insurance policies—some eighty million millennials are expected to make up 35% of all consumer spending a year.

Demand Models—Awareness, Preference, Decision, and Demand

Any sure-fire means to influence behavior is like the goose that lays golden eggs. Of the various attempts to manipulate others, to some, the best is a demand model, also referred to as a behavior model. There are multiple variations of demand models, yet each are designed to influence others to reach a predestined conclusion.

A demand model is a plan for communicating scripted messages over a series of stages. The model includes messages and when they are communicated. The demand model charts how a well-crafted message or messages or story line evolves and reaches its target audience. The demand model is a sequential rendering that moves targets from one stage to another to fulfill a designated purpose—such as joining an organization. They are used to influence a target market to models and are powerful tools.

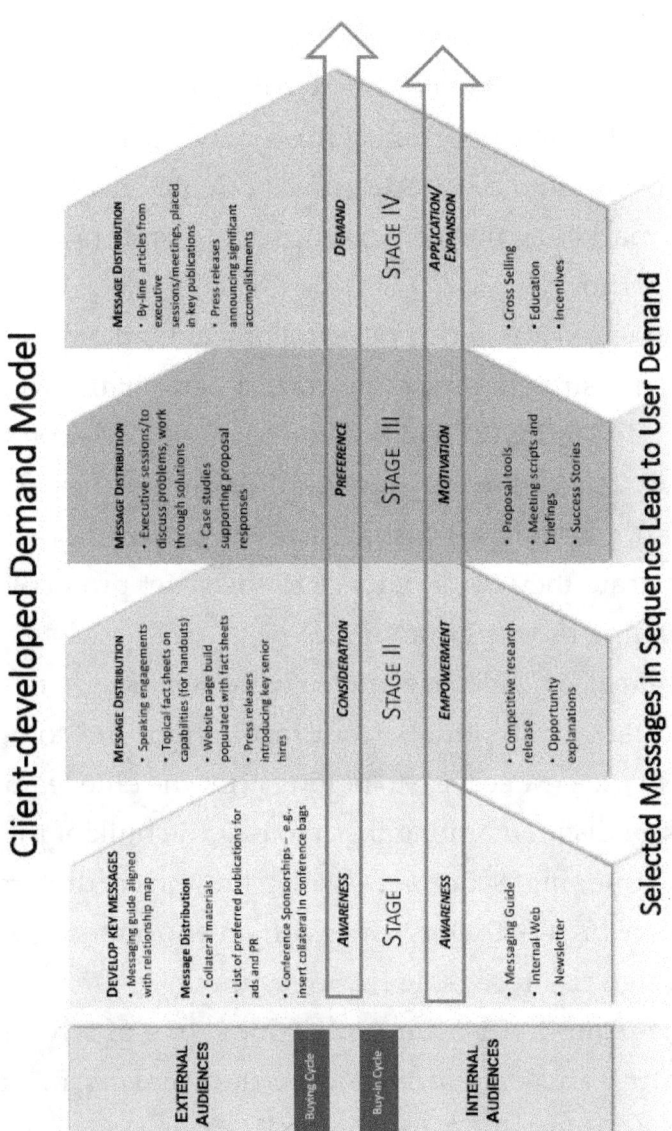

The demand model below is stripped of its messages, but shows the stages in logical progression. This one was used to solve a unique challenge which can only be described with a fictitious name, in this case, AZA.

The company, AZA, set aside approximately ten mil-lion

dollars to use within four years to launch a new Line of Service (LOS). It was hoped the investment would position the company for an opportunity for a new business offering in the aerospace industry. Executives calculated they could enter the market as newcomers, upsetting an established field of competitors.

The work was much more technical than anything AZA had demonstrated, and to be considered for the work, they would need to invest in a pool of talent whose expertise was narrowly focused in very technical disciplines.

Also, working against their favor, competitors could all demonstrate they could adhere to the strict protocols for accomplishing exacting standards.

Regardless, AZA executives were steadfast, and selected about twenty individuals from throughout the company to establish the new service. Not long after the elite team assembled, they decided among them to risk the bulk of the investment on one single contract—worth millions of dollars. It was a make-or-break-strategy, one with an enormous upside, but also a huge risk for losing the investment.

The team divided into subgroups, one of whose charge was to try and convince the decision makers in just nine months to select AZA for the work. It was also decided to communicate directly to targets and avoid tipping off potential competitors of the intentions of AZA executives to enter the market.

The outreach subgroup collected insights for personas to represent decision-makers and influencers. Each persona was populated with beliefs, aspirations, and expectations. The communications and communications channels were tested, and channels that could be repeated carried an evolving story line—along with feedback gathering.

Messages aligned to each persona made up the bulk of the effort, including the great care correlating the messages to demand model stages. As the plan unfolded, feedback was used for modifications to ensure targets were passing through the stages.

AZA beat out an established competitor for the work. The contract award was the largest win for the company in its one-hundred-year history. In time, the line of service became the most profitable business in the company.

Advancing Users Through a Demand Model

1. AWARENESS—The initial source of information communicated to members. Even if a member has existing awareness of the offering, proper direction will move him or her to the next stage.

2. CONSIDERATION—The promise of benefits, tangible or intangible, to drive users to weigh next steps. At this stage, members subconsciously determine cost-benefit trade-offs. Time could also pose a barrier to further consideration. Targeted messaging can convey benefits and create perceptions to reinforce positives.

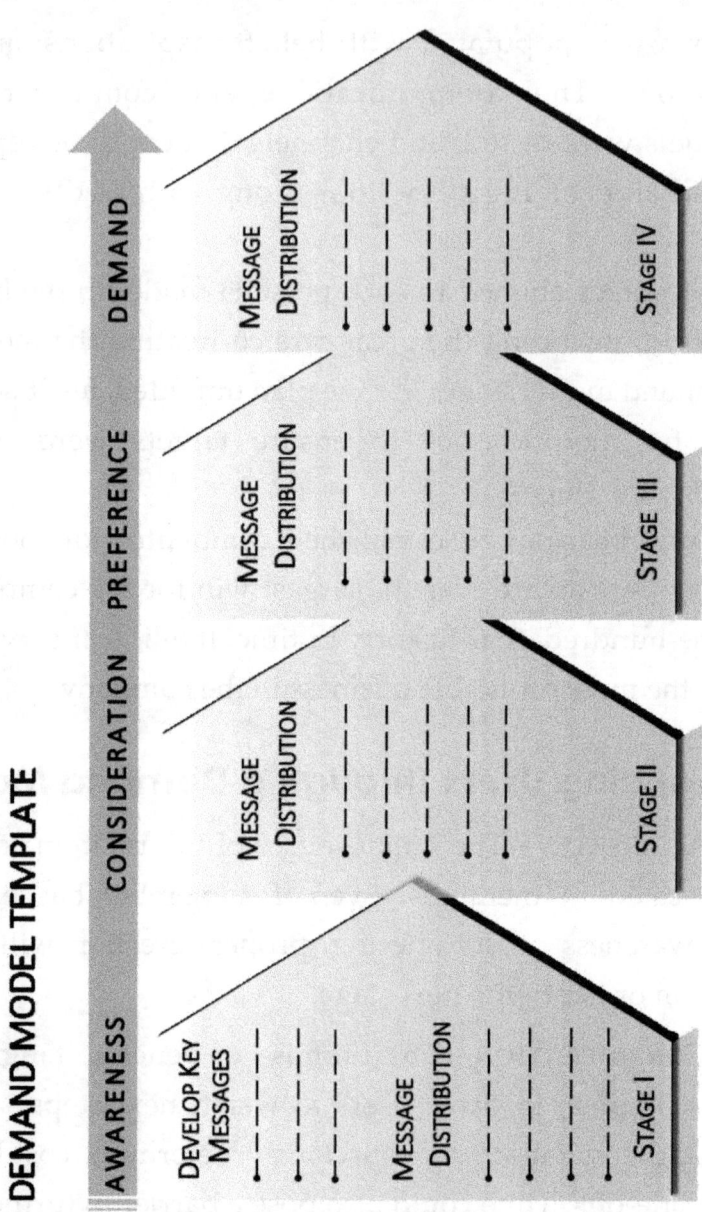

3. PREFERENCE—Members have decided they want or need your offering. They are likely to reinforce their decision by asking others for their opinions and probing details on the website along with other sources. Members draw

upon prior experiences for validation. This phase can be lengthened or shortened depending on the perceived value/cost.

4. Demand—The lower the cost, the higher perceived value of benefit. To arrive at this stage, the value has been properly communicated and perceived. There is a presumption the experience will be satisfactory. Organizations will do well to reinforce the benefits to offset any buyer's remorse.

VRBO Moves In

John Marshall and his wife, Pattie, have owned a vacation retreat out West for more than twelve years. They spend about three months there over the course of a year, and when not using their retreat, they open it up to renters.

For the first ten years, the Marshalls handled all aspects of their rentals from advertising to negotiating rates, arranging payment, and lining up maintenance and cleaning. The entire process for each arranged rental could transpire over days, weeks, and sometimes even months. Only about once a year would the Marshalls encounter a bad renter; but otherwise, it could be described as mutually satisfactory for both the renter and the Marshalls.

One day, out of the blue, the Marshalls received an email from the online advertising service they used, VRBO (Vacation Rentals by Owner). The email said the company would from then on handle the rental agreements, including contracts and money transfers.

The Marshalls had been subscribing to VRBO's advertising service for about ten years. They found it useful for promoting their property worldwide. VRBO has had a robust search function that renters can use to filter for destination, location, sleeping accommodations, and price. Renters were not charged for the service. Property owners, however, paid according to tiers of service around exposure of their property—its visibilities to perspective renters. The most expensive tier cost the Marshalls eight hundred dollars a year.

Over time, the top tier became a requirement, since all the other competitive property owners paid the premium price as well.

When VRBO's email landed in the Marshall's inbox, and after some teeth gnashing, the Marshalls realized they had no choice. They handed the transactions over to the faceless company.

After wrenching control, VRBO followed up with a new business model planting themselves squarely in the middle of the rental transaction as wholesalers. VRBO now required owners and renters to share the online company's fees. In less than twelve months, VRBO transformed from an advertising and match maker service to a wholesale realtor.

John Marshall described it as "putting a wrench in the middle" of their real estate business. What is more, the Marshalls were restricted in communicating with renters. VRBO explained the measures were to protect both parties against fraud. These messages were reinforced by VRBO through

Touchpoints along the process that the Marshalls and renters now had to follow, including cancellation policies, security deposits, and evaluations.

The new process was based on the notion of fraud, and messages stuck almost immediately. Renters came to demand VRBO's protection and were willing to pay VRBO 9% extra. John Marshall called the move "total disruption." The measures jacked up the costs of the rental, so the Marshalls must now charge more and earn less, and renters pay much more for VRBO's protection which is rarely, if ever, needed. No doubt some efficiencies arise from separating owners and renters from the transaction. Looking past them, though, VRBO has masterfully changed renters' beliefs, attitudes, and behavior—even among those who bring prior experiences.

The Marshalls recognized the shift in attitude among renters, who suddenly "were calling our cell phones at all hours to demand we refill soap containers, supply laundry detergent, and wondering why daily housekeeping didn't show," none of which were ever provided, John Marshall said. And, he added—somehow VRBO's messaging has been interpreted by renters in a way that blurs the distinction between a hotel with its front desk and concierge service, and someone's personal property.

Then there was the renter who straddled between the old and the new VRBO model. She discovered the Marshall's property on VRBO's site and went around the service to contact them and to negotiate rates, as was customary.

After the Marshall's agreed to the lower rate, the woman

balked at a security deposit, which is always required—whether through a PayPal account held in escrow, or through VRBO under identical conditions. But the woman told John her fear of being swindled to which he said in an interview that he was bowled over. His view, he said, was assuming the higher risk by handing his keys over to a stranger. "In more than ten years, and about seven rentals a season—that's a first.

REFERENCES

Aho, K. (2014, July 25). Geico Spent $935 Million on Advertising in 2013 and It Worked. Retrieved February 15, 2018, from https://www.bloomberg.com/news/articles/2014-07-24/geico-spent-935-million-on-advertising-in-2013-and-it-worked. Bloomberg News.

Claremon, B. (2012, February 22). The Inoculated Investor. Retrieved February 15, 2018, from http://inoculatedinvestor.blogspot.com/. Inoculated Investor.

Huetter, J. (2017, March 09). Buffett/Berkshire: GEICO saw big customer growth in 2016. Retrieved February 15, 2018, from http://www.repairerdrivennews.com/2017/03/01/buffettberkshire-geico-saw-big-customer-growth-in-2016/. Repairer Driven News.

Holodny, E. (2016, February 27). Warren Buffett thinks

GEICO will be Americas No. 1 auto insurer by his 100th birthday. Retrieved February 15, 2018, from http://www.businessinsider.com/warren-buffett-thinks-geico-will-be-top-spot-when-hes-100-2016-2. Business Insider.

Kestenbaum, R. (2017, June 14). This Is How Millennials Shop. Retrieved February 15, 2018, from https://www.forbes.com/sites/richardkesten-baum/2017/06/14/this-is-how-millennials-shop/#71ba7de244ce. Forbes.

Quinn, R. C. (2017, March 24). The Power of Branding Through Catchy Advertising, GEICO Commercials. Retrieved February 15, 2018, from http://www.ipwatchdog.com/2011/02/24/the-power-of-branding-through-catchy-advertising-geico-commer-cials/id=13081/. IP Watchdog.

Chapter IV – Be Memorable

"Spotify is embracing service design as part of its move from a music streaming service to a music brand that's more about lifestyle than a particular product."

Ben Davis

@Econsultancy

8 – USER EXPERIENCES

Experiences are real and occur, and there is a process for an experience to unfold. That process is based on forming preconceptions, which are critical for judging an experience. Our preconceptions become the criteria and standards we use to determine satisfaction.

> **Experience**
> *noun*
> Practical contact with and observation of facts or events.
>
> *verb*
> 3rd person present: **experiences**
> Encounter or undergo (an event or occurrence). "The company is experiencing difficulties"

Few businesses match the advantages of cruise lines to influence behavior through memorable, satisfying experiences... so passengers, hold on to your wallets. The cruise lines are dedicated to entertaining vacationers with activities that satisfy passenger needs. That requires creating preconceptions, and monitoring and evaluating experience outcomes for possibilities to improve before the voyage ends.

Passengers, meanwhile, are wholly receptive, even eager, for memorable experiences to occur, and remain open to messages doled out along the way. For instance, entertainment directors will use popularly attended gatherings to ask passengers to count aloud the number of cruises they have taken. In the background, staff cheer on those who have cruised the most.

What better opportunity to influence an ideal target audience than holding them captive in an artificial environment and bombarding them with incentives to keep on spending over the length of a voyage.

~ ~ ~

Sitting in a Starbucks recently, I was explaining to a colleague the meaning of a service experience, and thought of the coffee company's business model. Customers come in with a preconceived idea of what to expect. And that expectation is either satisfied, or not. In other words, it's either a positive or a negative experience.

We all take some comfort when our expectations are met. Conversely, if you have ever walked out of your favorite restaurant dissatisfied, the experience didn't live up to your expectation. However, anyone who has visited a Starbucks, even once, will find the experience similar to any one of the other twenty-eight thousand stores worldwide. The coffee retailer relies on décor, flow, and arrangement to create a comfort level. Subconsciously, we all crave familiarity, which leads us to establish routines. As we grow older, we tend to gravitate toward even more familiarity in our lives, steering away from situations that we might find awkward or confusing.

With Starbucks, our expectations are met the moment we walk through the door. From any vantage, the retail shop is familiar with recognizable patterns that lead us through a predictable experience. We know where the line forms, have an idea what's in the glass case, can quickly scan the menu, and can manage the Italian-English jargon to order. And when we screw up, there's always a forgiving barista.

I've noticed that, often, some of the very same people who disparage Starbucks coffee are also regulars. They are not likely to bolt—neither due to costs or convenience—unless there's an alternative that meets their need for a familiar, comfortable, reliable, friendly, positive experience.

Satisfying expectations keep customers coming back. A service that continues to underwhelm, on the other hand, will not survive.

Back to the Starbucks demonstration. My colleague, whose timing was superb, responded: "Ah, then if what you say is valid, Starbucks is missing an opportunity if they fail to ask its customers whether their expectations were met."

Well, it just so happens, when I got home—no fooling— I had an email from Starbucks asking about my experience.

~ ~ ~

"That was so unsatisfying, I'll never come back." Jack Johnson said after spending thousands of dollars on a company dinner. Johnson, a senior executive was so dissatisfied with what he was served that the next morning he instructed his administrative assistant to make sure he never again had a meeting there. "It just did not match my expectations," he told me.

How is it that a McDonald's burger, fries, and shake are satisfying, yet a meal prepared by a master chef using the finest ingredients fails to impress? Even more, our experience at a McDonald's doesn't seem to be marred by rude order takers, unsanitary bathrooms, or rowdy Cub Scouts. The distractions and inconveniences—which one can anticipate—has little impact on what is otherwise a consistent, reliable experience.

How can there be any commonality for comparing these two services? The answer—because, it reflects our preconceptions for what to expect with a service. In the above scenario with Jack Johnson, the outcome was contrary to what should have been a hands-down win for fine dining. But it turns out each of us sets expectations that we rely upon to measure experiences. McDonald's is consistent and our expectations are typically satisfied. Ultimately, we all take away impressions from experiences. These accumulate in abstract references, residing somewhere between our conscious and subconscious, which we later use for decisions.

We use our expectations to sort, rank, and prioritize abstract references, psychologists and researchers say. As a result, we can offer an opinion of an experience, yet barely describe or define it to others. Nafiz Imtiaz, a marketing executive at a California-based communications company, suggests our expectations are shaped by exposure and interpretation of our environment, price, points of comparison, and any combination of them all.

EXPECTATION INFLUENCERS	DESCRIPTION	SHAPING	FEEDBACK TYPE
EXPLICIT SERVICE PROMOTION:	• Communications: environment, price, points of comparison, or a combination of all three.	• Reflect the actual service versus aspirational.	• Accuracy of service as expected?
IMPLICIT SERVICE PROMOTION:	• Cue, such as price, experience.	• Price levels/premiums justified by increased levels of performance versus member needs, tastes and attitudes.	• Check incentives against other services or competition.
WORD OF MOUTH:	• Rely on promoters and advocates, and respected opinion shapers.	• Use of prominent testimonials.	• Determine NPS "promoters."
PAST EXPERIENCE: (PARTICULAR SERVICE) (WITHIN THE SAME INDUSTRY) (RELATED SERVICE)	• Capture feelings and expectations of prior experiences.	• Use of input from feedback for improving or designing next program.	• Did your service meet expectations? What were your expectations? What stood out as meeting your expectations? (Importance on a scale of 1-to-10).

Serving Up Satisfaction Deliciously

Le Relais de l'Entrecôte which translates to steak house in English, is known for its steak-frites throughout France, with locations in Paris and elsewhere. The restaurant attracts locals and tourists who wait no less than an hour for a coveted seat among the one hundred or so per sitting.

The business model is the epitome of predicable consistency, for which diners can be assured of having their expectations met. The restaurant's menu hasn't changed since 1959—steak frites, a house salad, and a few choices for drinks and dessert.

Even while writing this, I can summon the experience: spirited conversations in line; no-nonsense, efficient service; and above all, the Parisian-infused tastes of garlic butter.

By narrowing choices and defining the boundaries, l'Entrecôte is able to deliver dependability which is then replicable and thus scalable. With little room for error, I would only imagine dissatisfied diners are rare.

Unlike in the United States, Europeans don't mess around with success, thankfully. But if l'Entrecôte were to fuss with its menu, it would result in disaster of untold proportions. Its entire business model would need reconfiguring.

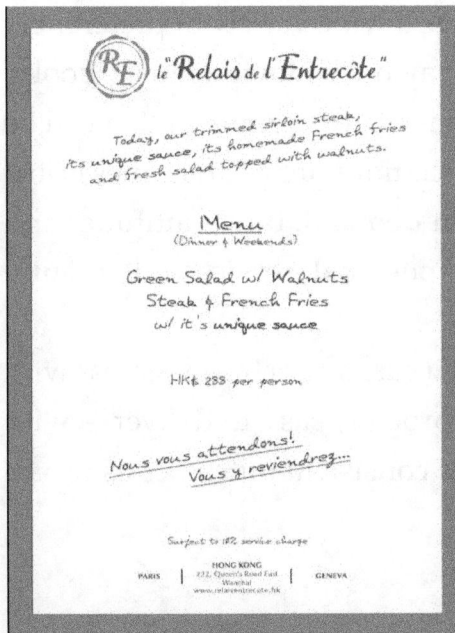

The restaurant would need new staff training, new equipment, and would need to stock greater varieties of ingredients. But perhaps most of all, the change would introduce degrees of unpredictability.

l'Entrecôte demonstrates that a service is sufficiently successful when users are merely satisfied. Once expectations are met, users interpret an experience as positive. So, it's somewhat ironic that some executives will strain resources to do even more. They act as if meeting expectations is barely a passing grade—nominally satisfactory, the minimum threshold.

How often do we come across an organization whose core value statement runs along these lines: "We strive to exceed expectations?" This thinking is a recipe for failure. Imagine for a moment the kind of organization that exceeds members' expectations. What kind of operations would that take? It might be possible to ask what each member's expectations are and deliver exceptionally. But exceeding expectations would require increasingly higher levels of satisfaction, which if not implausible, is incredibly resource-driven.

Services that accommodate a wide variety of preferences are difficult to scale. iTunes may offer movies, music, books, and such, but they are all forms of entertainment that can be streamed. Moreover, the expectations are clear. iTunes is just a conveyance for streaming on-demand. But as attitudes and behavior constantly shift, a personal service will require tighter constraints.

Executives, also, will find it easier to achieve success with an offering that is simple to process, easy to deliver— with limited choices—and achieves consistent outcomes as promised.

9 – USER JOURNEYS

Searching "Journey Maps" on Google results in fifty-seven million sites. Among them were consulting companies, marketing firms, tool vendors, and bloggers. From just the top sites, few would assume a journey map is simply a two-dimensional diagram that could be sketched out with pencil and paper. To service designers, moreover, journey maps are like a Swiss army knife in that there is no right or wrong configuration. The right Journey Map is the one you find most useful.

Journey maps show the sequence of a user's interaction with a service. They can be developed with observations of users' patterns, and with input from survey research. Their value is determining norms and user expectations which can then be intercepted for achieving satisfactory experiences.

Journey maps were conceived by service designers hired to improve the experience of train travel. The journey map guided service designers in ways that led to redesigned platforms, railcar designs, down to bathroom reconfigurations, and ergonomic arm rests.

Designing an Acela Experience

It took nearly ten years from when Congress authorized a high-speed train service in the Northeast corridor to Amtrak finally rolling out the Acela. The concept was to create an efficient transportation service for thousands of commuters, largely based on the Shinkansen Bullet train in Japan which snakes through the countryside between major cities passing by Mount Fujiyama at up to one hundred fifty miles per hour.

At the time, Amtrak was struggling to overcome a reputation of unreliable service. Among first-time riders, fifteen percent complained to survey researchers in 1989 saying they would never again travel aboard Amtrak. The company's president, George Warrington, said, "If Amtrak can reduce that rate by one percentage point, its revenue would rise by thirteen million dollars a year."

Long past a time of romanticism, traveling by rail in the United States had become a chore; it was slow, uncomfortable and expensive. Major airlines, meantime, were shuttling commuters at a cost of fifty dollars one way, between Washington, New York, and Boston every hour on the hour, with a guaranteed seat—no passenger would be left behind at the gate if a flight filled up, even if that meant flying one passenger on an otherwise empty plane.

Amtrak could barely fill its trains along mid-continental routes. Under any other circumstance, Amtrak, a for-profit, would have been long gone. But federal officials insisting a national rail service was in the country's best interest, subsidized each ticket sold by about five dollars, or roughly one billion dollars a year to maintain operations.

With the Acela, the first high-speed rail service in the Americas, Amtrak would leverage the introduction to try and cast off its suffering reputation. While one could argue the company had nothing to lose, it spared little expense pulling out all the stops to rebrand with a new logo, matching uniforms, and its own traveler guarantee: any dissatisfied passenger would be eligible for a "make-good" free train ticket.

But Amtrak did not stop there, the company decided to invest in Service Design for a new-improved rail experience.

 The challenge offered to service designers from IDEO and C+CO was to improve the existing experience. Their solution was a journey map to understand the rail experience from the traveler's perspective. The designers reasoned that the journey began when travelers first considered their options and weighed those against their needs and journey ended as an experience well after the traveler disembarked. Using surveys and observation, the service designers then mapped a traveler's journey to improve the experience, giving birth to the journey map.

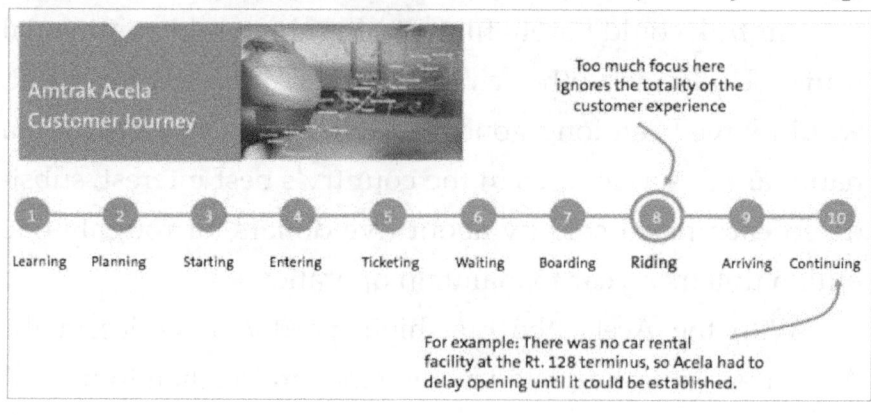

Each journey is depicted in a continuum so designers can see how experience unfolds from the user's vantage. In addition to planning the ideal experience, the maps reveal any service gaps. These are often filled—for a smooth experience—with improved communications, better process, and fixed technology.

However, a journey map has a short shelf life. The input is just a snapshot in time and place. Using similar means for inputs, such as new observations and survey results, a journey map could come out very different. The maps are subject to any number of variables, perhaps impacted by the economy, trends, and even individual circumstances. The vendors who wind up on Google's search engine sell more precise correlations for journey maps—using behaviors, geo-tracking, computational analysis, and dashboard outputs. Some vendors go so far as to monitor multiple personas, manage access points in real time, and recommend new paths for a satisfactory experience. The greater sophistication these vendors offer is in response to those who argue users rarely follow a linear path through a service.

Before turning to a vendor, it would prove useful to tackle a journey map in-house, if for nothing else than to realize the perspective from a users' point of view.

Journey Map Template

Stage	Awareness/Discovery	Consideration/Research	Decision/Purchase	Post-experience
Touchpoints				
User Experience				
Actions				
Motivations				
Questions				
Pain Points				
Overall Satisfaction				
Customer Experience				
Recommendation				
Ideas for Improvement				

10 – BLUEPRINTING A SERVICE

A service blueprint, a schematic of sorts, is used to show the workings of a service—how users and providers must interact for a positive result. The blueprint is a means for service designers, program managers, functional departments, executives and other stakeholders to communicate with each other. The model helps satisfy the need for everyone involved to recognize their role in helping a service transpire. Before their service blueprints, the efforts to build new services were prone to repeated failures.

In short, blueprints help:
- Choreograph user experiences
- Isolate points of failure—work solutions offline
- Use and improve technical capabilities to automate, improve experiences

There is a storied Department of Defense chart—perhaps as renown as the purple water fountain in the basement—used to visualize a sequence of activities that must occur for building advanced weapon systems. These include jet fighters, aircraft carriers, and tanks, to name just a small sample of what the military would procure. Upon first appearance, the chart resembles one of those modern art pieces that stretch credulity. But to engineers, project managers and others, this schematic plastered along walls, which end-to-end could likely wallpaper the entire ten-square miles of the District of Columbia, is a pattern of systems engineering V-Models which to those who have the right training, is quick to decipher.

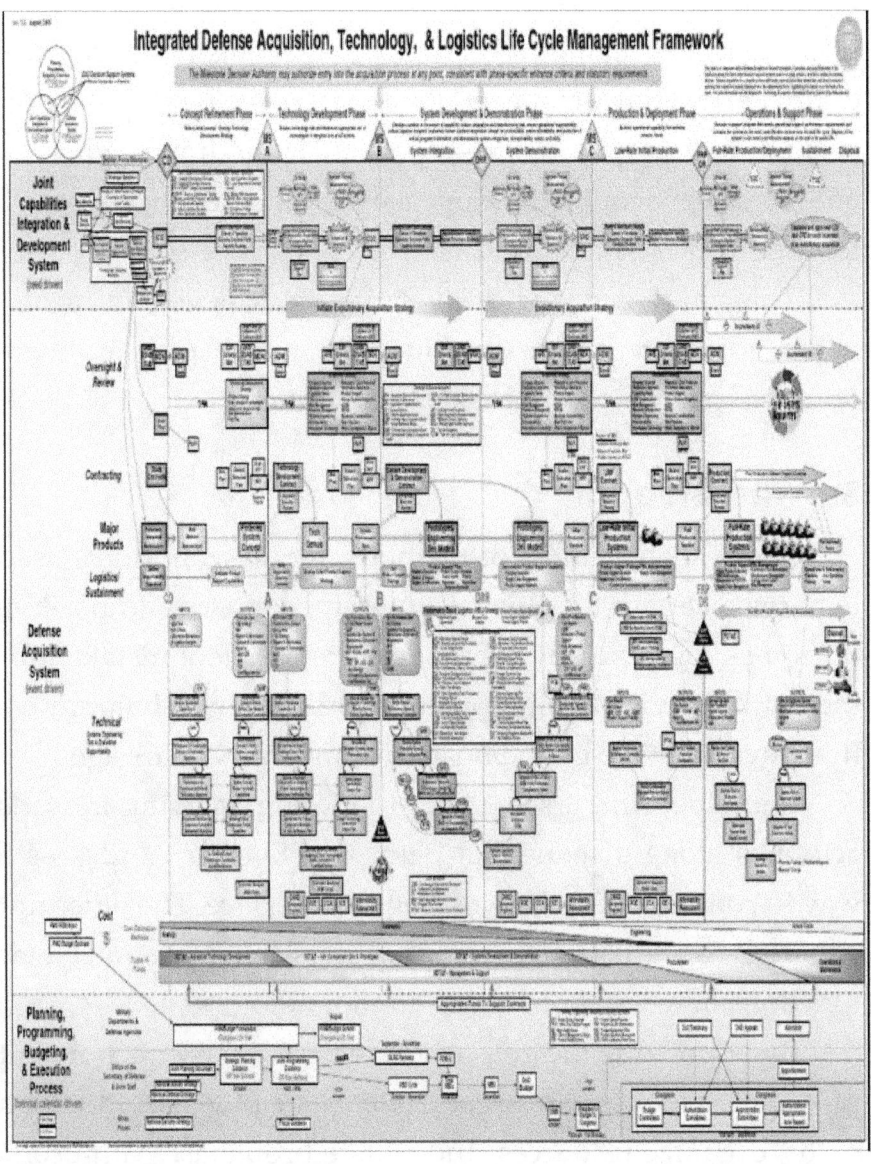

As an aside, I thought initially the chart was someone's idea of a joke, mocking the complexity of government process. But in time, I too came to recognize the brilliance of visualizing the complexity of milestones, gates, team, and organization responsibilities and where to delineate activity from decision-making. Without the acquisitions chart, I doubt very much anyone would could easily identify the progress of a weapon system—a particular hindrance when an entire system acquisition can easily extend beyond anyone's tenure.

This chart was obviously quite an achievement to develop. Fortunately, a service blueprint, which achieves much the same purpose, is far easier to construct.

Service Blueprint

There are a number of methods, models, and tools used in Service Design to achieve successful services and positive outcomes. But none of the models are as often mistaken for the entire Service Design practice as the service blueprint—first devised by G. Lynn Shostack some thirty years ago.

The blueprint, a schematic rendering showing a user's activities along a sequential path, was Shostack's idea as a way to communicate the workings of a service. The blueprint is simply an illustration for providers to orchestrate their functions in response to users' commands.

By visualizing the give and take between user action and provider response, an organization can plot user decision paths, organize resources, and isolate problems. With users' as the primary focus, organizations can build better programs that result in satisfactory experiences.

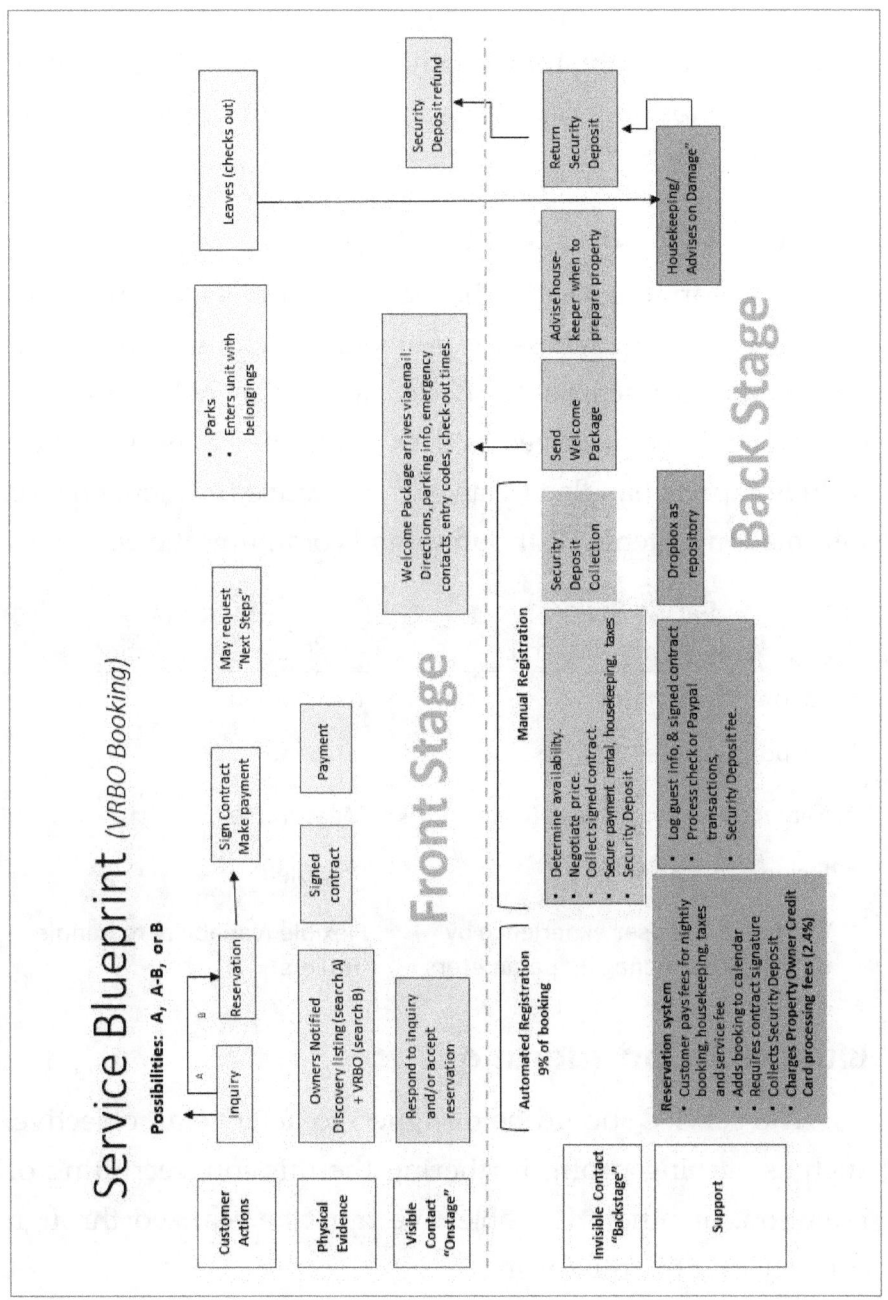

Service Blueprint *(VRBO Booking)*

As an example, a user seeking access to a member benefit could trigger a series of responses, from an automated message and redirection, to options for choosing individual-based selections, obtaining further information, access to coupons, or a shopping cart. With a blueprint, providers can plot each sequence.

Front Stage and Back Stage

A blueprint is divided between a Front Stage—the user's actions, and Back Stage—the provider's responses through its organization's functions. The Back Stage, mostly hidden from users and could be described as back office operations, will likely include aspects handled by an administrative function, finance, information systems, distribution, and communications.

FRONT STAGE (Experience Delivery)	BACK STAGE (Process Components)
• To user satisfaction	• Transparent
• Responsiveness	• Efficient
• Minimize-eliminate gaps (usability)	• Measurable
• Include Touchpoints	• Reliable
• Challenge the user experience by defining and managing parameters	• Flexible (capability to handle outliers)

Blueprint Considerations

The service should be designed to achieve an objective, such as earning profit, furthering the mission, recruiting or retention, or other. The objective must be realized through constructing the Blueprint.

- **Timeframes:** Since all services depend on time, set a threshold for each step.

- Boundaries: Establish the parameters for experiencing failure (and revise with subsequent experience-lessons learned).

- **Service Delivery:** Since personnel play a fundamental role in service delivery, work to gain their buy-in through collaboration and proper training.

- **Technology Needs:** The organization's needs are determined in part by requirements from the Blueprint.

Buying into an Experience

The online superstore, Amazon, provides individual experiences for shoppers based on data the company collects on each shopper. From account-based activity, to tracking your computer activities, Amazon amasses data on each customer to create a custom online experience. This follows Amazon's service concept: "Customer obsession rather than competitor obsession… and operational excellence"—which aligns to how the site responds to user actions, and influences the entire transaction.

Amazon collects each shoppers' search history, page views, wish-lists, written and observed reviews, and of course, purchases which are translated through algorithms. This activity, which occurs even when we are not on the site, is to influence users from when they sign in. Over time, experiences more closely align to users' tastes.

Designers responsible for creating these experiences orchestrate a carefully crafted process to: 1) Expose shoppers to a wider range of products and services (based upon their demonstrated interests), 2) Provide levels of comfort to reduce any amount of reluctance, and 3) Speed users to and through a purchase, according to Webdesigner Depot, a blog.

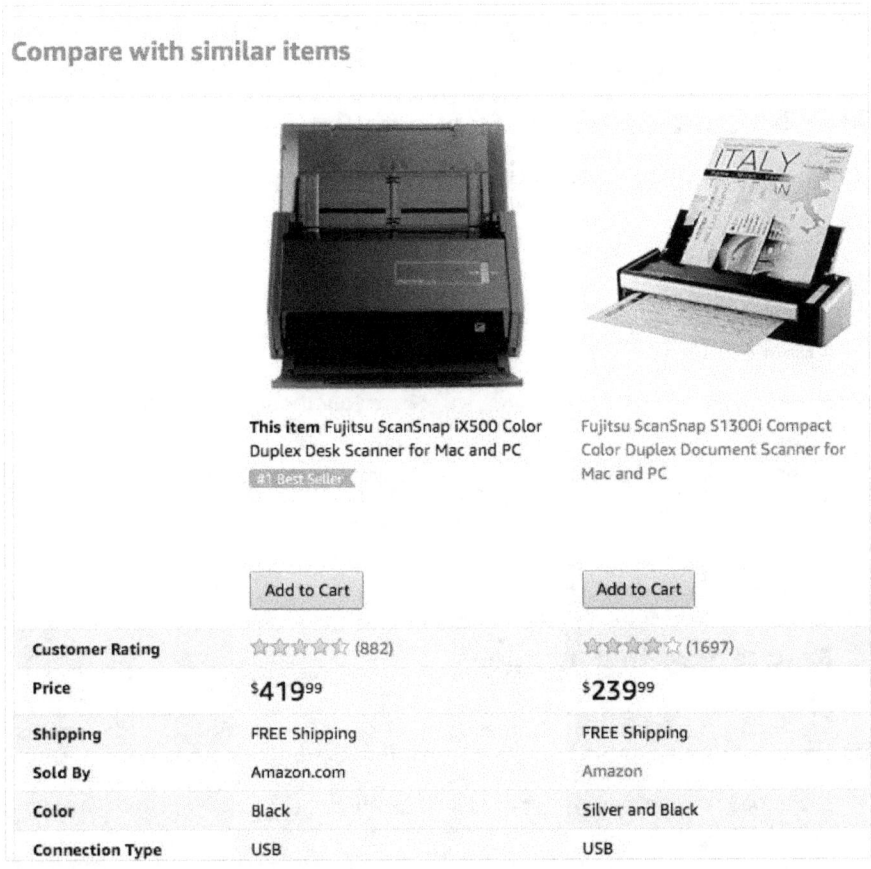

Compare with similar items

	This item Fujitsu ScanSnap iX500 Color Duplex Desk Scanner for Mac and PC #1 Best Seller	Fujitsu ScanSnap S1300i Compact Color Duplex Document Scanner for Mac and PC
	Add to Cart	Add to Cart
Customer Rating	☆☆☆☆☆ (882)	☆☆☆☆☆ (1697)
Price	$419⁹⁹	$239⁹⁹
Shipping	FREE Shipping	FREE Shipping
Sold By	Amazon.com	Amazon
Color	Black	Silver and Black
Connection Type	USB	USB

Exposure to Other Products and Services

The custom landing page on Amazon includes a variety of navigation opportunities prioritized by visibility. Buttons are colored with gradients and 3-D effects. This **was** designed to help users who are uncertain with how to proceed. Additionally, hovering over the button "Shop All Departments" triggers a drop-down menu showing departments for searching Amazon offerings.

The navigation bars are always in view, "where users

expect to find them," say the authors of "An Analysis of the Amazon Shopping Experience." The search function is intuitive, bringing up results from singular and plural queries in addition to other items that could be a logical match.

From the "product page," shoppers can check out or add the item to a wish list for later. The product page nearly always includes photographs that enlarge. Scrolling farther down are suggestions based on what others bought. And even farther down is detailed product information and user-submitted reviews. Algorithms also help to bring shoppers back to where they left off next time they sign in, from any of their devices.

Speed Users' Checkout

As shoppers add items to their cart, a banner might appear if they qualify for free shipping. And even before hitting "order this item," shoppers can change or delete the number of items, plug in an address, change, a payment method, and save a payment method for future one-stop-checkout. An email follow-up confirms the order which can be canceled any time before shipment.

Chapter V
Disruptive Innovation

"Successful companies want their resources to be focused on activities that address customers' needs, that promise higher profits, that are technologically feasible, and that help them play in substantial markets."

Clayton M. Christensen
The Innovator's Dilemma: When New Technologies Cause Great Firms to Fail.

11 – EXPLORING TOUCHPOINTS

Steve Jobs continually experimented with Touchpoints to try and create experiences that would persuade customers to buy the company's products. The first attempt was a cyber cafe for consumers to learn about Apple products over a Danish and coffee. But the food and beverage service was difficult to manage, and besides, it took the focus way from Apple. The next foray turned out to be the now-ubiquitous retail stores, a venue chock full of touchpoints.

A touchpoint is a provider's opportunity to interact with users at any intersection of communications. Often, they are used as gateways for providers to nudge users along an experience which includes soliciting feedback. Touchpoints flow through websites, social media, emails, direct mail, phone, in-person meetings, in-store visits, and packaging—to name a few.

As for Apple stores, they are designed as an entire experience, guided by touchpoint messages continuously bombarding shoppers—consciously and unconsciously—as they wander through the store. Apple seeks to convince shoppers to adopt the Apple lifestyle. To that end, it obviously requires owning Apple products.

The experience begins at the front door from where shoppers oversee a clean, uncluttered space, welcoming those who might otherwise be intimidated by interacting with a plethora of the most innovative, powerful, sophisticated machines on the planet. Shoppers who wander in find widely spaced-aisles lined with long tables and pull-up bar chairs and carefully created spatial patterns arranged in ways that personify easy navigation. Throughout there are smooth textures, open spaces, and bright illumination. Strategically-placed cues lead shoppers to desire a lifestyle embedded with dynamic music, vivid videos, and exciting exploration made possible with finger gestures and a single-touch. The stores outside the states riff off the locale's art, history, architecture, and culture.

Apple Store Touchpoints Around the World

If you are a traveler and have missed visiting an Apple store in, say, Amsterdam, London, Paris, Shanghai, Hong Kong, Sydney, or Prague, you have might have missed out on a worthwhile experience. Many of the stores, ranging from the size of tennis courts to Olympic pools, are architectural representations of the host cities. Here is one blogger's list of the top ten Apple stores.

1. UAE: First Arab world store: A mall location with the familiar Apple theme plus the addition of green trees.

2. Regent Street Store, London: An historical Edwardian Period look. Inside, magnificent glass staircases, a glass bridge and dazzling illuminated glass ceiling.

3. Fifth Avenue, NYC: The once-upon-a-time toy store F.A.O. Schwartz, made famous in "Big" and other movies, is now an Apple store—and remains an attraction. Sometimes thousands of visitors queue up around the thirty-two-foot glass tube entrance for a look inside. The store also occupies one of the most iconic locations, on 5th Avenue, across the street from The Plaza Hotel-on the southeast corner of Central Park.

4. Opéra, Paris: The storefront is a one-hundred thirty-year-old-building; inside is mosaic, brass, and stone work in French romantic style. Some say the look strays too far from a typical Apple store.

5. Ginza, Tokyo, Japan: This is Apple's tallest store, a stainless steel and glass structure. Inside, an elevator with no buttons carries passengers between floors.

6. George Street, Sydney: Known among enthusiasts for the largest Apple logo and the largest Genius Bar.

7. Boylston Street, Boston: Boston is home to Apple's largest U.S. store and is a recognizable landmark with its enormous glass walls. In addition, there is a garden rooftop, which unfortunately remains inaccessible.

8. Upper West Side, NYC: This store, known for its unique triangle-shaped glass and stone structure is the only store situated in the busy downtown area, and is yet unattached to any other building. It remains the most expensive store in Apple's real estate portfolio.

9. Shanghai, China: To enter this store requires descending a floating glass spiral staircase from the main floor of a crowded shopping mall. The stairs lead customers underground to a circular store carved out of the foundation.

10. Carrousel du Louvre, Paris: Located near I. M. Pei's glass pyramid in the center plaza of the Louvre; this two-story shop is in the shadow of the building housing the Mona Lisa and other priceless art. Of note, there is a stunning spiral staircase between floors, constructed of glass to appear as if it is floating in the center of the store.

Apple has their eye on further deepening shopper experiences by intensifying touchpoint sensory perception. The stores are adding indoor vegetation, touch-sensitive displays, impressive videos, and ways to fool the eye for the true sizes and shapes of the stores.

Building an Experience

The diagram below suggests where to insert touchpoints in a user experience, and their purpose. Touchpoints are based on messages, which when crafted in a sequence as shown in the diagram, can evoke emotions and motivate behavior.

Providers use touchpoints to shape user's experiences: their uses can range from creating expectations, to developing themes, to soliciting feedback.

GUIDE TO TOUCHPOINTS

INPUT-OUTPUT	PROVIDER OUTPUT	USER INPUT	PROVIDER OUTPUT	USER INPUT
	Communications: Email, Fliers, Word Of Mouth, Website, etc.	User actions: Visit website, attend conference, booth visit, e.g.	Reinforce: Continue the service.	Expectations met? Positive Experience? Satisfied/not?
HOW USERS SHOULD PROCEED direct users to realizing needs	Call to action	Learn expectations - monitor user activities	Motivate action	Satisfied?
SHAPE EXPERIENCE through communications messages	Communicate expectations	Find out if expectations on track to be met	Reinforce key messages	Determine satisfaction
IMPROVE Did experience meet needs-preconceptions?	Devise feedback loops – acquire insights that can be used to improve	Gather, accumulate responses	Communicate improvements in process, or completed	Gather metrics to monitor service impact

Identifying Touchpoints

User interactions can be real or virtual—such as online chats to company support, which nowadays can appear as if there's a real person on the other side. That is until the answer to your question is too generic or out of context. Along those lines, one tends to wonder if companies measure the reactions of users, and whether there are a good number who feel foolishly deceived?

Meantime, the insurance company, State Farm, had for years relied on an automated phone system in place of an operator. But since recent memory, the company shifted to live representatives. While it may wind up costing more per call to have a live person on the other end of the line, in my mind it has to offset any ill will caused by customers circling through an abyss of preprogramed call line directories.

In other words, claimants already distressed by a loss, will tend to be more loyal customers when they reach a human who is supportive and reassuring.

- SETTINGS (PLACE): Many communications to users are direct—providers to users. Providers can shape experiences and control them through the way services are delivered. Does a user have to complete a service at a booth, in a classroom, or online? And if online, how does that evolve? The atmosphere, the mechanics, the responses—all of these can be, and should be, controlled. The growing service industry frequently includes a mashup of other providers. A Learning Management System (LMS) is delivered to members through a web service, and plays a surrogate role in delivering the service. Whether the LMS is branded to your organization or not, it has a role communicating to members. It provides the setting for Touchpoints as a second party. UPS and Amazon partner to deliver purchases in ways that allow both to keep their brands. The multiple advantages are UPS has a built-in stream of business and Amazon's customers have access to full-service packaging from tracking to ease of returns with printed labels and drop off facilities. FedEx TechConnect is an example of an unbranded partnership, a business line for an air freight company, rumored to repair leading brand electronics along runways at strategic hubs. The customer is under the impression that its repairs are in the hands of the manufacturer.

- **PROCESS AND TECHNOLOGY:** Touchpoints exist along workflows where process brings together (integrates) people, place, and technology. Online technology is partially process. For example, Progressive Insurance quotes its prices online.

Online Approaches to Touchpoints Online

EVOKE EMOTION:

Coastal Conservation League—This website uses beautiful photography to evoke emotion.

~ ~ ~

ENGAGE AND INTERACT:

The Teachers Guild – A Center of Excellence.

The site has been built around the user:

- Who are you?
- What is your interest?
- How can we help you?
- How can you contribute?

Each page is arranged around someone's interest in a lesson topic, with a highly interactive community sharing resource and collaborating on ideas.

~ ~ ~

UNCOVERING INTERESTS:

National Association of Retirement Plan Participants.

Hovering over an image reveals a question, and clicking the image takes you to the answer. Through a series of queries, feedback, and further response, NARPP's interactive website matches individuals to needs, and identifies the staff responsible for following up.

~ ~ ~

- **THE EXPERIENCE:**

ALS ASSOCIATION

With large call-to-action boxes on the ALS Association website along with photography and large vector icons, this website uses provider output touchpoints and user input to display only the most relevant content, to prevent overloading, or overwhelming users.

~~~

- **OPEN COMMUNICATIONS:**

National Geographic.

High impact visuals, uncluttered typography and scrolling
pages offer a large canvas to view National Geographic's
world-renowned photography. But also, there are comments
to the side for establishing expectations: "Next week, we'll introduce our new video player. Fair warning: The site offi-
cially launches on Monday, so in the meantime you might
run into some bumps. Be patient as everyone is working hard
to complete the move as quickly as possible."

Touchpoint: All Wrapped Up

Georgetown Cupcake owners Katherine Kallinis and Sophie LaMontagne are known to hand out up to one hundred free cupcakes to the first one hundred customers who respond to their promotions on Facebook and Twitter.

The two sisters, former reality TV stars from the TLC cable show DC Cupcakes, opened up Georgetown Cupcakes in 2008 on a corner along M Street in Georgetown, Washington, D.C. There was a time when the TV show and their store were synonymous.

There are better cupcakes in town, locals say. But there is a cache about Georgetown Cupcakes that attracts many to lineup along the side street and wait their turn to enter, including tourists.

"Cupcakes aren't about taste, they're about lifestyle, and that's where Georgetown Cupcake has it nailed," Laura Sloat, Vice President of Content Strategy at Delucchi Plus, wrote in a blog post.

Georgetown Cupcakes is distinguished by pioneering an approach to packaging. Some might call it clever brand-ing, but its packaging communicates the idea of gifting, hence it is a touchpoint. It is not terribly difficult to find a bakery in nearly every large city specializing in delicacies. When

 bought as gifts, they are received as a gestures of kind-ness. But with Georgetown Cupcake's, its packaging of cupcakes also connotes a de-gree of class.

It could be argued that most distinctive packaging is post purchase reinforcement, displaying a brand and hint-ing at the value inside. With Georgetown Cupcakes, it is the other way around. The packaging, perhaps the most distinctive aspect of their

business, is the first thing one sees when they enter the store. Besides which, in this instance, the packaging is worth more than the sum of its contents.

"It's about the tell-tale pink boxes with their black-and-white stickers—boxes that look chic when delivered as birthday presents, or when sent to offices," Sloat said. "Cupcakes are locked into place, arranged all in a row, with 'perfectly symmetrical frosting swirled just so' every time. For the young (primarily female) urbanites who flock to the store (and spend upwards of fifty dollars to ship the cupcakes cross country), this is not about indulging a sweet tooth, it is about cachet; it is about the fondants, the TV show, and Us Weekly."

There are, of course, other companies using packaging for messages. "Tiffany's is considered number one," Kim Peterson of CBS MoneyWatch said. "The robin's egg-blue box is so beloved that the company now sells a tiny version of it as a $250 charm. The box has inspired table centerpieces, wedding decorations, and party cakes."

Added to the list is the candy company Russell Stover, whose lingerie box is a top hit for its heart-shape and black lace covering. "The box quickly became one of the company's best-selling products," according to BusinessWeek.

And then there's Apple that conveys practical functionality and design in every product and service that carries its familiar name and logo. Products are encased in sturdy white cardboard, with accessories cleverly tucked into form-fitting plastic inserts. The Apple store bags are also see-through so others can admire and desire others' purchases.

Does anyone else have great difficulty throwing away the well-designed packaging from an Apple product? It just seems like an affront to all those who were involved in its design, packaging, and care in delivery.

TOUCHPOINTS USED BY TOYOTA TO SELL THE YARIS

TARGET YOUTH MARKET:

- **Awareness:**
  Yaris was featured in the *Prison Break* television series, which appealed to younger views and their tastes.
- **Consideration:**
  Toyota followed up from its initial airing by sponsoring an interactive contest for the best three-minute television commercial.
- **Preference:**
  The car was integrated into television comedy programming with sponsorships and advertising.
- **Purchase/Decision-Making:**
  Yaris cars were rolled out during youth-oriented events, particularly those that were organized around the use of social media.

(Source Shimp, 2005, c2009)

REFERENCES

Andrews, J. C., & Shimp, T. A. (2018). Advertising, promotion, and other aspects of integrated marketing communications. Boston: Cengage.

Peterson, K. (2014, October 09). 10 of the world's most iconic packages. Retrieved February 15, 2018, from https://www.cbsnews.com/media/10-of-the-worlds-most-iconic-packages/. cbsnews.com.

Sloat, L. (2011, December 15,). Cupcakes: A Case Study. Retrieved February 15, 2018, from goo.gl/UFQPF1. kglobal, a division of Zenetex.

Zia, A. (2015, November 17). The Top Ten Awe-Inspiring Apple Stores in The World. Retrieved February 15, 2018, from https://www.igeeksblog.com/top-ten-awe-inspiring-apple-stores-in-the-world. IGeeksBlog.com.

12 – INNOVATION STARTS HERE

Technology is a catalyst and accelerator for change, influencing trends, attitudes, tastes, and expectations. We can anticipate change, and we can assume change, but we can't know its result, plan for its impact, or know exactly when change has occurred.

In the hands of a service designer, technology can help disrupt markets, deliver program benefits, shape user experiences, and capture emotions.

Technology allows two-way communications, setting parameters for process, and automating service delivery. Recognizing that the pace of technology will only increase, organizations should be sufficiently nimble to act and react in ways to remain relevant

~ ~ ~

In the span of just three decades, advanced communications and Information Technology have fundamentally altered the ways executives think about organization sustainment and growth. On one hand, organizations pursue technology for such benefits as creating a competitive edge, efficiencies, greater capabilities, and to employ strategies for growth—what could be innovation.

On the other hand, to use the technology calls for individuals with the right set of skills. When the technology first emerged, few had the needed skills, but even more, there was no established measure to assess competency. This created great uncertainty in employment. Executives were scrambling to figure out ways to staff up their technology—hiring the right skills at the right costs, in sufficient numbers to adequately operate the organization's technology.

The gap in determining skills and competency fell to associations whose members would collaborate on establishing bodies of knowledge. These, then, became the standards for measuring competency, providing industry sectors with the confidence to hire the right skills at the correct competencies and pay the employees what their skills are worth.

Those standards also served to identify the requirements for what individuals would need to advance in their fields. These requirements could be offered as revenue-generating opportunities for associations: certifications, training, publications, seminars, and the like. Additional revenues allowed associations to hold down increases in fees and also provide a robust portfolio of value-added membership benefits.

The tech boom, though, had a wide-reaching impact on not just new careers and career opportunities, but also on businesses that would launch to exploit technology for helping organizations innovate and grow.

In the not-too-distant past, the path to employment success for the best and brightest would be fairly predictable. Students from the best schools were likely to be hired by large, established, prestigious companies, the likes of, say, International Business Machines Corp. (IBM), JPMorgan Chase

& Co., McKinsey & Company, and Goldman-Sachs. Those hires who showed the most promise were continually tested with challenging assignments, offered opportunities for formal mentorships, and supported for continued education which sometimes was required for advancement.

The growth in technology, however, threw that prescription up in the air for anyone who thought they could use technology to innovate. They had to have ideas for where technology could advance society, arguably the seeds to disruptive technology. The incubator for ideas known as startups now became familiar concepts. And those who pursued that path were regarded with the same awe that had once been reserved for those hired by Fortune 500s.

Yet succeeding at a startup meant trading off financial security and long-term stability for the uncertainty of succeeding as an entrepreneur *and* innovator. Those who timed the market with the right innovation would reap enormous wealth seemingly overnight. Joining a start-up also had great appeal to scores of young, newly-minted professionals who lacked the hard skills and ideas, but nonetheless jumped at the opportunity to learn and grow with the technology.

Against that backdrop, the larger, staid companies found themselves wrestling with a new generation of workers whose loyalty didn't necessarily transfer to an employer. This forced a rethinking of how to maintain a competitive edge using human capital; determining how to lure the most talented individuals for roles at various levels, and ensure the success of rising up to positions of leadership. So companies began to cut back on resources for career growth.

Again, professional membership associations took on the role for filling professional development gaps on behalf of their members. Beyond networking, associations could serve as the source for learning, keeping current, stretching their skills, and finding mentors.

~ ~ ~

As I reflect on the changing landscape resulting from advancing technology, Michael Beekley comes to mind—someone I knew from elementary school. Beekley (not his real name), typifies the experiences of some who dove into a startup to experience the ride. Still in his early thirties, with admittedly limited IT skills, he took an opportunity to learn as a junior computer coder working at a newly formed company—America Online (AOL). In exchange for a decent salary, he agreed to partial payment in stock options. AOL's shares were trading at about fifty cents.

Beekley met his wife Annie there, and she, too took a portion of her salary in AOL stock. Low and behold, founder Steve Case timed the market with great aplomb, capturing millions of subscribers within a nascent Internet, offering a complete web experience through an exclusive platform. With some familiarity of Case's story from those who helped him during the early stages—he was both the entrepreneur and innovator, betting on a technology that he helped develop, and was later abandoned, by GE Information Services.

After just six years of experiencing the company's growth from startup to the largest internet service provider on the planet, Beekley and wife found themselves owning a pile of shares now worth $90 each, a growth of eighteen thousand percent over what they were worth when they both started work at AOL. So Michael and Annie, who had sacrificed lower wages for years, cashed out, becoming instant millionaires. At that point, they quit their jobs and left the world of work behind — retiring permanently before their fortieth birthdays.

Other newly minted millionaires, among them Elon Musk, went on to try again, forming new companies with new ideas; some that have become exemplars of innovation whose technology is having wide impact on society, our everyday lives, and our nation's economic performance.

The Experience of Rides on Demand

For those who have wondered why the design of cars has basically remained unchanged — hold on tight. At the 2017 Consumer Electronics Show in Las Vegas, the North American International Auto Show in Detroit, and at Service Design meetings around the world, the buzz is all around how Service Design will help satisfy the needs of a booming on-demand ridership market.

Big thinkers are predicting it will not be long before drivers opt-in and decide to trade out private vehicle ownership to services operated by the likes of Uber, Lyft, and others. After all, who wouldn't want to relinquish the costs of insurance, gas, and maintenance, along with the ever-nuisance of parking.

The shift is already in gear. Roughly forty million passengers rely on Uber for their transportation, according to Uber Statistics, an independent research organization. Competitors, including Google and Intel-owned Mobileye, have joined in testing vehicles with a focus solely on satisfying passengers.

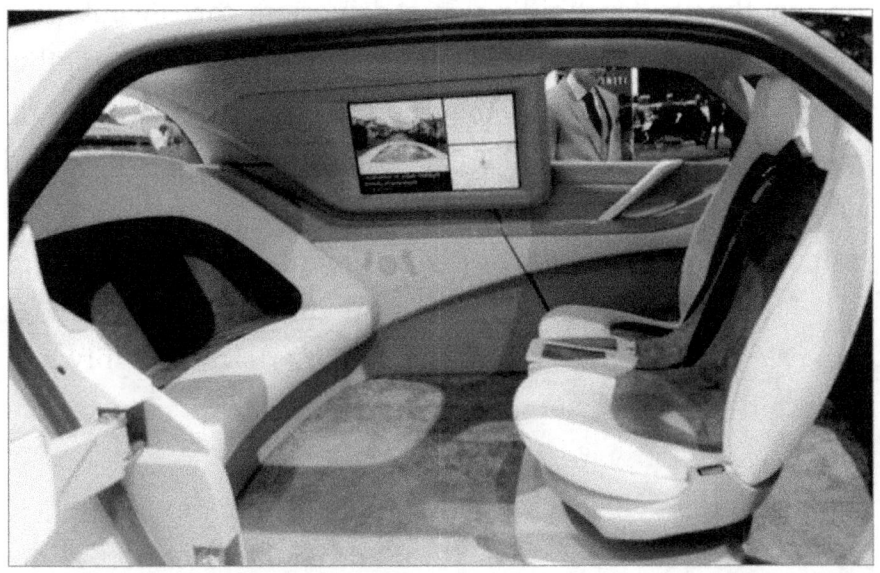

"Our company's brand 'The Ultimate Driving Machine' is in jeopardy," Holger Hampf, head of Customer Experience Design at BMW, said while speaking at a recent Service Design Network Conference. "The vehicle of the future will cater to those who may never sit behind a wheel."

Some of the techniques of Service Design will be used to plan how riders call up the services with ways to prevent the experience from failing. This will occur by service designers configuring the service process to balance the needs of companies and their customers. To be sure, riders are likely to choose their preferred ride-on-demand service based on the one best adept at Service Design.

Getting to Trust

Drivers surveyed in a recent poll were somewhat mixed on whether to trust riding in a driverless car. Twenty-five percent of respondents said they had no concern; another twenty-five percent said they had no opinion; and, the remaining fifty percent balked at the idea. The poll, conducted nationwide between Jan. 29 to Feb. 1, 2016, by Morning Consult, has a margin of error of two percent.

The respondents were even more united over concern for driverless vehicles sharing the road with drivers. Eighty percent said they believed there would be "glitches in an autonomous car's software."

Driverless vehicles, also known as autonomous, refers to vehicles that can operate without human intervention. Autonomous vehicles are not limited to cars. The technology has been tested successfully on underwater vehicles with flying drones. Still, the automatic default with automobiles remains semi-autonomous--already available in varying degrees on most cars sold today. These include automatic braking, lane control, self-parking, and more, with added features and improvements coming out each model year.

So, while we are willing to rely on semi-autonomous features with us behind the wheel—maybe even distracted— will we come to trust pure autonomy? And, if so, how will we achieve a transition to trusting the technology, particularly given the predisposed opposition presented in the poll results?

~ ~ ~

Some of the most successful service providers—whose names will be familiar—Apple iTunes, Amazon, and PayPal have amassed one billion credit card account numbers from consumers, according to a study published by Quora.

Where consumers were once reluctant to provide email addresses and cellphone numbers to even, say, local favorite restaurants for discounts, nowadays most consumers rarely think twice before sending credit card numbers and other personal identification over the internet. It has been shown by repeated surveys that shoppers nowadays turn to the internet to shop before entering a store. In all, some 190 million Americans shop online.

What's more, fewer consumers are expressing any reservation for engaging in financial transactions that require interacting with faceless service providers.

ComScore, a media measurement and analytics company, regularly samples respondents who make at least two online purchases every three months. They report more of us are storing financial account numbers and passwords on our phones and tablets—devices most vulnerable to those who seek our personal data. In 2016, 47% of shoppers used smartphones for their purchases, devices most vulnerable to those who seek to know our personal information.

Have we become complacent about our security online, or

have most of us decided to choose convenience? Either way, online service providers have become quite successful in convincing us that convenience, ease-of-use, and familiarity outweigh the risk of exposing our personal, financial data.

This discussion is not to advocate for increased security measures, but to illustrate an attitude shift that has occurred during several years. It is generally understood consumers who do not adopt additional preventive security measures are consenting to share their personal data online, so long as it causes no financial harm.

Now, consider that online brands had to win over our trust, a prerequisite for influence. Moreover, they were constrained by messages and channeling them online through the internet. So how did these companies convince us to shed our fears? In short, they took opportunities to learn our behaviors, promulgate trends, and fill consumer needs or create needs that needed filling. Learning our behaviors and monitoring our responses is how the companies created acceptance for us to conduct financial transactions online.

The availability of increasingly sophisticated technology certainly helped tip the balance toward trust. But swift marketers pushed the comfort zone with incentives, messaging, and price discounts aimed at luring consumers to shop online.

Marketers acquire feedback from cookies often unsuspectingly planted on our computers; and watch our online habits and preferences using "trackers" that follow our online activities. Even more intrusive, our contracts with service providers allows them to share our computer addresses, geographic location, and browsing history. What little else remains unknown or out of reach to companies and advertisers can be asked via surveys. The information, by the way, is often relayed in real-time, which is how advertisers are able to position ads on other sites we come across while browsing the internet.

Advertisers seek to determine ways to motivate which messages will alter our behavior. Some advertisers test us with coupons in hopes of learning our price point for switching brands. Others, at any time, want to know how far consumers will travel to redeem a coupon. These messages are found as pop-ups in some GPS apps and devices.

To be sure, this is not about stealing, or causing harm; it is how we can be convinced to part with our money.

~ ~ ~

Once trust has been established, executives must now compete for loyalty. This involves finding the issues that appeal and lure with calls to action. There are few limits to influencing users. But it must proceed with insights into users' interests and tastes—better still, knowing the lengths of their passion.

In the future, expect to be influenced in more ways that are pervasive and less noticeable. These influences will occur with greater ease and comfort from using technology. In addition, expect information to be more tailored, immediate and relevant. And while many may continue to weigh security over convenience, the entire conversation will be mostly subsumed by prior consent—and not necessarily with an individual's conscious acquiescence.

Preventing Overload

It was not that long ago that some predicted great benefits to our intellect from technology. A handful of prognosticators even claimed that access to near limitless information would fundamentally change our species. We were supposed to gain greater intelligence by access to more information. But that thinking has ceased.

"Although there is considerably more information with which to deal," Harvard researcher Joseph Ruff said, "our brain's ability to absorb and utilize this information is no better suited for us than for the people who lived four or five hundred years ago."

Behaviorists say our minds can keep track of five-to-nine items at time, and once we have reached our threshold, we shut down, no longer capable of forming judgements.

Taken to the extreme—merely to demonstrate--there are some among us who are unable to synthesize much information at all, often classified by behaviorists and psychologists as having a processing disorder. Those at this extreme find life very challenging, unable to make even simple decisions. The majority of us, however, will most likely come to say: "I'm just too overloaded to deal with that right now."

Malcolm Gladwell, the renown New Yorker magazine writer and author of *Tipping Point, Blink* and other best sellers, wrote about Campbell's Soup Company and their struggle during the 1980s to compete against Ragu spaghetti sauce. In Gladwell's recounting, Campbell's called on a famed researcher, Howard Moskowitz, to help the company figure it out.

Surveying scores of consumers, Moskowitz discovered shoppers were overwhelmed by the more than 40 different offerings of Prego sauce on store shelves. So shoppers were prone to shut down and choose among Ragu's fewer choices instead. Moskowitz wrote in his analysis of findings to scrap all but three flavors. Within months Prego topped the market, and of its mix of new choices, Chunky became a market leader, responsible for six hundred million dollars in earnings in its first year.

The Value of Algorithms to Solve What Our Minds Cannot

Those who earlier expressed doubt about the relevance of information technology and communications to lead economic growth need consider how algorithms serve as the secret sauce to many service successes.

Within nano seconds of a keyboard command, an algorithm, perhaps in tandem with other algorithms—searches the world's accessible data drawing from billions of bytes residing on multiple servers thousands of miles apart constructed by an assortment of manufacturers, then ranking, and sorting the results into meaningful ways, based on the users input—delivered to the users' onscreen browser in, say, a second to two.

So, those whose measure of progress is by whether a robot is able to replace humans, they might want to reconsider how we measure progress along with the tools for advancement.

Today we use algorithms to perform hundreds of millions of instant stock trades; and for guiding an average 100,000 flights a day along their routes—bringing passengers safely to the ground. We also use algorithms for love, as a way to search and find our mates—a two-billion-dollar service industry. And for our safety, algorithms help to monitor and predict terrorist activities using feeds based on networks and communications.

Yet even in light of the sophisticated capabilities and seeming complexity, developing an algorithm is accessible and affordable. As for scale, algorithms can help accumulate and sort user information, even given greater value personas and journey maps by using the insights to serve needs and predict behavior.

Watch Apathy Disappear

There was a time when critics of Netflix were betting on which month would mark the end of its new video streaming service. This was in 2007, at a time when Netflix offered its mail-order customers the opportunity to save six dollars a month by moving their subscription over to streaming. Many of its customers, including Annie Loeb, took up the offer, assuming they would have continued access to Netflix's extensive catalogue.

Annie was jazzed by the concept and began collecting lists of titles to watch, which she hoped to add to the queue as she had done previously as a mail order customer. Then, she discovered there was no queue, nor did the online service carry any of her preferred choices. "I wanted to quit right then and there," she said. "But my family convinced me to wait and see."

I, too, found Annie's experience perplexing. So, I dug in only to discover it wasn't just Netflix who had this problem; Pandora, Spotify, and other online entertainment services were also constrained by having to pay artists for streaming. This forced the companies to balance between satisfying subscribers and carrying the smallest catalogue possible, which could appear larger by rotating titles in and out. For these reasons Netflix faced customer churn in alarming numbers, and simply stacking up titles for customers to browse and choose wasn't working. In a paper widely circulated on the Internet, two Netflix executives described their challenges and ways around them.

"A typical Netflix member loses interest after sixty to ninety seconds spent reviewing titles," wrote its primary author, Carlos Gomez-Uribe. "The user either finds something of interest, or abandons the service." Not until Netflix discovered algorithms, with capabilities to shape expectations and influence decision-making did the company vault back to the lead of the movie-rental market.

Netflix uses a number of algorithms, some that keep track of customers' choices, others to manage its catalogue, and others to recommend titles to customers. Over time, its recommendations become more refined, reflecting customers' preferences and taste.

Google, too, uses algorithms for validating and verifying searches. Company researchers also travel the globe finding untapped markets to survey demographics for data to add to the algorithms for improving search results. Google also depends on algorithms to stay one step ahead of those who sell internet search optimization services to companies, which according to a 2016 study has become a sixty-five-billion-dollar industry.

The importance of algorithms cannot be overstated. The technology has been responsible for one of the largest and most recognized global companies, Google.

"Think back on every fear, every hope, every desire you've confessed to Google's search box and then ask yourself: "Is there any entity you've trusted more with your secrets?" Esquire contributing author Scott Galloway wrote, "Does anybody know you better than Google?"

Larry Page and Sergey Brin launched Google to solve a growing need among internet users—more reliable search results, more quickly.

The two devised what they called PageRank, a series of algorithms to "crawl" the internet for matching titles, headings and fields, along with meta tags embedded in programing code. PageRank then sifted through the data in what's known as indexing, and sorted the final results for better reliability based on cross-reference mentions of the findings.

By contrast, one of its early competitors, AskJeeves, relied on human editors to match user queries, then sorted the final results by the number of visitors or hits. Most search engines at the time measured order of importance based on website visits. In due time, anyone who professed to be a search engine optimizer was gaming the results by merely having a group with internet access to repeatedly land on a particular website.

The story of Google is now similar to many other high-tech startups. Two college students came together with a similar idea in 1996 and soon after found early investors. In Google's case, Larry Page, a University of Michigan student was touring the Stanford University campus for graduate school, and met his student tour guide, Sergey Brin. Together they founded BackRub whose name was changed to Google in 1998.

During Google's first fifteen years, the company's annual revenues did not reach $1 billion. However, five years later, from raising capital to invest in growth, its revenues soared to $5 billion—due in part to the growing number of internet users worldwide.

Five years on, in 2013—the company's revenues surpassed $50 billion, 36% more than the year before. And in the third quarter of 2013—during just three months of reporting earnings—Google's internet business zoomed to $15 billion, of which $10 billion accounted for revenue from advertising services.

Today, Google has to remain innovative, in a constant drive to stay ahead of competitors. Analysts value the search engine market (SEM) which is in excess of $70 billion a year. Google has 74% of that market. Its nearest competitor, Baidu—who most internet users have probably never heard of—has just 10% of the market—65% less than Google. The remaining SEM companies are eager to take on Google for a greater market share.

To that end, Google must keep changing its algorithms. For one, it must keep relevant. An approach Google uses is sending researchers around the world in search of new markets, collecting data from demographics that can be fed into algorithms.

For two, it changes its algorithms to stay ahead, to foil would-be hackers. Consider, there are an average 3.5 billion users who query Google every single day—that's 1.2 trillion searches worldwide a year. Anyone with insights into how those algorithms rank searches would be worth untold millions of dollars to those who aspire to have their website content at the top of searches. All these efforts are to ensure Google remains the dominant market share leader.

More recently Google has expanded beyond advertising services to offering consumer products tied closely to mobile devices—the fastest growing access point to the internet.

REFERENCES

Alphabet Inc. (2018, February 13). Retrieved February 17, 2018, from https://en.wikipedia.org/wiki/Alphabet_Inc. Wikipedia.

Frommer, D. (2014, August 19). Google's growth since its IPO is simply amazing. Retrieved February 17, 2018, from https://qz.com/252004/googles-growth-since-its-ipo-is-simply-amazing/. Quartz Media

Galloway, S. (2018, February 13). Silicon Valley's Tax-Avoiding, Job-Killing, Soul-Sucking Machine. Retrieved February 17, 2018, from http://classic.esquire.com/silicon-valleys-tax-avoiding-job-killing-soul-sucking-machine/. Esquire.

Mangles, C. (2018, January 30). Search Engine Statistics 2018. Retrieved February 17, 2018, from https://www.smartinsights.com/search-engine-market-ing/search-engine-statistics/. Smart Insights.

Search Engine Market Share [Advertisement].
(n.d.). *NetMarketShare*. NetApplications.com.

Chapter VI
Measuring, Testing, Prototyping

"A design isn't finished until somebody is using it."

Brenda Laurel, designer at MIT.

13 – TESTING

Whenever there are changes to tax law, I am drawn to wondering how the Internal Revenue Service deciphers the legislation into the forms U.S. taxpayers are required to complete. While the tax forms are simply a tool designed to determine the total tax due to the government, each entry box and line is based upon an interpretation of the law.

I picture a team of mathematicians, accountants, and systems thinkers diagramming the forms—beginning with the law and working backward from the applicable schedules—the topic sections. Sheets are added for schedule-based line items that require more computation and detail. Yet, since the schedules must apply to any number of unknown variables and circumstances, the team's work requires extensive testing. The consequences from failure can be enormous, with the possibility of substantial costs and lost time, as courts decide disputes that could remain unsettled for years.

This is not at all insignificant given the complexity of the task—handling the large numbers of individuals, corporations, and other entities involved; using software that aids individuals and accountants; and the managing of large, small, and frequent dollar amounts. Additionally, thousands of government workers must provide the back-office support in comport with process and standards, and a technology interface.

It almost goes without saying, all these interactions present enormous opportunities for failure. Minimizing the risk requires extensive, ongoing testing.

Testing What You Owe in Taxes

CONSTITUTE REPRESENTATION

- **Congressional Branch:** Passes the laws that form the basis for federal taxes: who pays, what is taxed, and a percentage base.

PUBLIC COMMENT PERIOD ON PROPOSED RULES

- Executive Branch:
  - Interprets the laws.
  - Proposes and issues rules and regulations to comply, publishes and distributes rules, instructions, and forms.
  - Processes, enforces, and adjudicates.
    - Processes: reviews, collects sums, archives.

DISPUTE RESOLUTION PROCESS

- **Judicial** Branch: Adjudicates disputes, complaints, and challenges for any part in the process.

Does Your Certification Program Measure Up?

A variation on the SWOT Analysis (Strengths, Weaknesses, Opportunities, and Threats Analysis) is an organization Program Assessment Model (PAM). The model offers a careful examination of your personnel, finances, capabilities, goals, and whether problems are worth fixing. PAM requires identifying critical internal and external factors (above), and running them through an assessment to determine the health of the program.

Traditional SWOT Analysis

STRENGTHS, WEAKNESSES, OPPORTUNITIES, AND THREATS

A SWOT analysis is a common exercise in organizational strategy. The analysis requires identifying and examining internal and external factors—and selecting and evaluating those most relevant to attaining the intended objective.

Traditional SWOT Analysis
Strengths, Weaknesses, Opportunities and Threats

A SWOT analysis is commonly used for organizational strategy. The model requires identifying internal and external factors that could lead to success or failure.

STRENGTHS	WEAKNESSES
- Internal advantages	- Internal disadvantages
- Factors contributing to success	- Needs,requirements for improvement

OPPORTUNITIES	THREATS
- External market opportunities based on changing demographics, trends, attitudes, and tastes	- External disadvantages - Barriers

---

Both the SWOT and Program Assessment Model rely on identifying internal and external influences. The Program Assessment Model, however, is far more rigorous. Based on a tool used by management consultants, the model reveals each aspect of the service system, using an approach that delves deeply into the system operations, functions, and activities. Its thoroughness ensures nothing is left unrevealed and un-reviewed.

The figure below was used to evaluate a certification program. From the top working downward, the governance overview begins with the Board and its overarching role of program strategy and overview, including goal setting, establishing guidelines, resolving disputes, budgeting, quality control, and determining improvements.

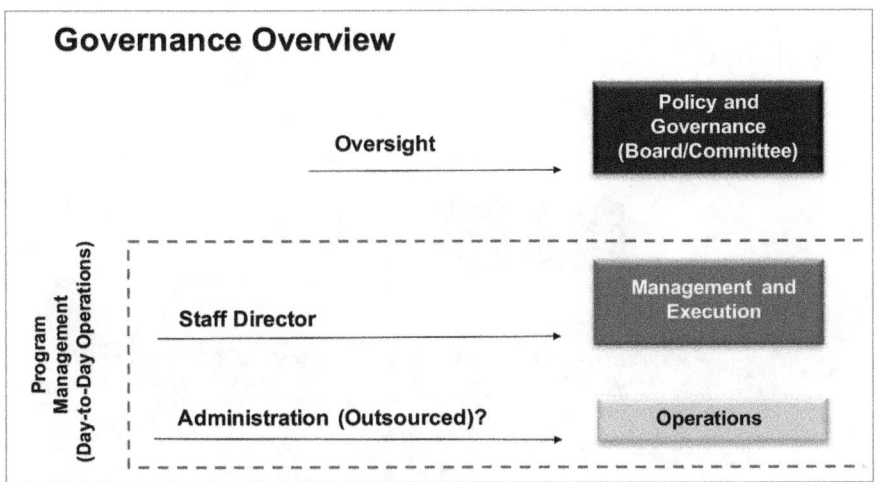

Just below, the senior program manager is identified with responsibilities for "management and execution" and "operations," reports to the Board.

The management and execution operation is isolated below.

Within management and execution, the major activities are depicted in an organization chart.

The model below is used for evaluating the overarching activities of management and execution. To the left is a listing of activities. Across the top row is scoring. As the scores accumulate, they total to the right as a snapshot, showing the health of activities, including improvements needed.

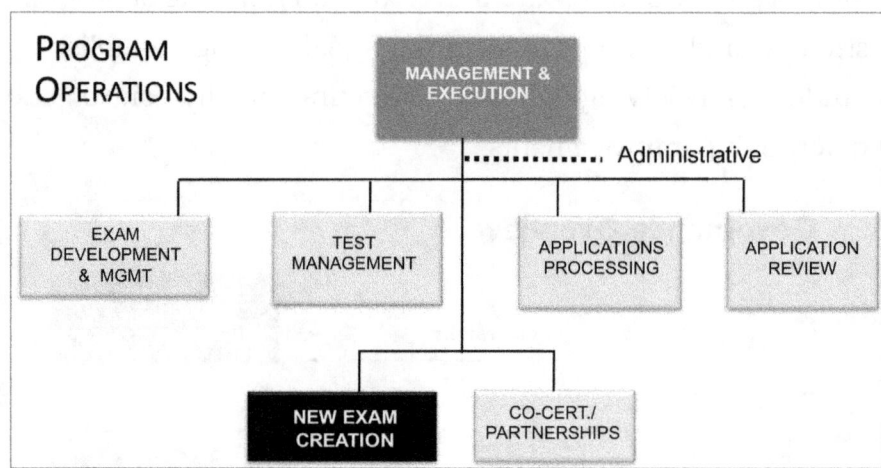

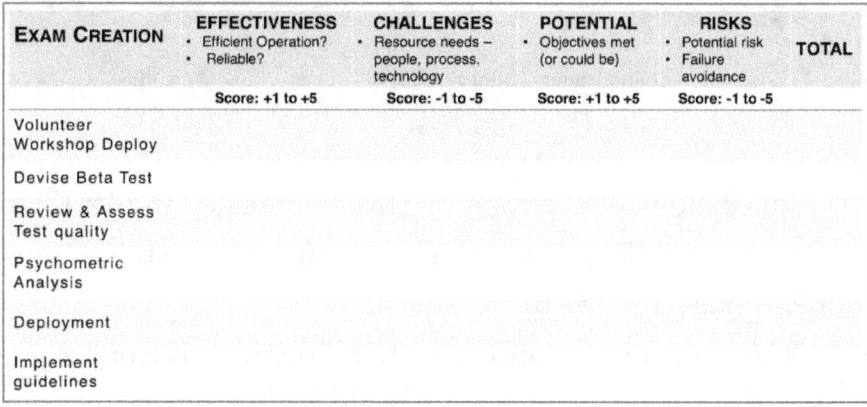

EXAM CREATION	EFFECTIVENESS • Efficient Operation? • Reliable?	CHALLENGES • Resource needs – people, process, technology	POTENTIAL • Objectives met (or could be)	RISKS • Potential risk • Failure avoidance	TOTAL
	Score: +1 to +5	Score: -1 to -5	Score: +1 to +5	Score: -1 to -5	
Volunteer Workshop Deploy					
Devise Beta Test					
Review & Assess Test quality					
Psychometric Analysis					
Deployment					
Implement guidelines					

For more detail, the model below shows the function of New Exam Creation by separate activities. This example is real, for which the program manager and members of the board determined the primary activities.

New Exam Creation

- Workshop
- Review
- Beta Test Prep
- Psychometric Consulting/Analysis
- Test Publish and Deployment
- Analysis
- Roll-out/Website/Communications/etc.

The program assessment model for exam creation includes some of the list above—yet no scores are included. The thinking for not adding scores to the examples is to reinforce the role of evaluators, so they determine the correlations for themselves.

EXAM CREATION	EFFECTIVENESS • Efficient Operation? • Reliable? Score: +1 to +5	CHALLENGES • Resource needs – people, process, technology Score: -1 to -5	POTENTIAL • Objectives met (or could be) Score: +1 to +5	RISKS • Potential risk • Failure avoidance Score: -1 to -5	TOTAL
Volunteer Workshop Deploy					
Devise Beta Test					
Review & Assess Test quality					
Psychometric Analysis					
Deployment					
Implement guidelines					

Scoring and Scoring Factors

The program assessment measurements gauge effectiveness, possible challenges, future potential, and looming risks. The use of pluses and minuses for the tallies help identify those activities requiring attention.

- Internal factors:
  - Effectiveness: Are operations effective and most efficient; functionally reliable—operated by qualified people using preferred technology?
  - Challenges: Are resource needs met—where does failure occur, might occur?
- External factors:
  - Potential: Are organization objectives met; do objectives require reevaluating—perhaps ahead of meeting emerging, expanding opportunities?
  - Risk: What are costs, politics, social factors, and technology that could cause decline, eventual failure?
- Factors for Consideration
  - Environmental scan review:
    - External
      - *Political:* Regulations...
      - *Economic:* How the overall economy can impact an audience.
      - Social and Cultural: Trends: Changing attitudes, tastes—demographics such as increase, age distribution, and segmentation.
      - *Technological*: Progress, significance, sufficiency

of automation; rate of technological change, shifts, and costs; quality, and lead to innovation.

- Internal
  - □ Existing strategies, particularly those aligned to environmental factors.
  - □ Strategic issues involved in the development of a corporate plan.
  - □ Critical success—the achievement of objectives and strategy implementation.
  - □ Assessment product/service life cycle. This is best determined using the Growth–Share Matrix.

Growth-Share Matrix

The Growth-Share Matrix helps to determine whether to invest in improving a service. The model, known variously as BCG, was created in 1970 by Bruce D. Henderson to analyze product lines based on cash-flow. There are four quadrants for earnings vis-a-vis market share.

- Cash Cows have a large market share for a service with stagnant growth. At times, large meetings and conferences fall into this category. These are services with steady, predictable income whose revenues exceed costs. The services in this category should be maintained but not improved with investments in hopes of growth.
- Dogs are considered dead-ends—services that attract little interest or demand for which there is little likelihood of future growth. Perhaps the offering is mature, tired, or found elsewhere for better value. These programs may break-

even, but even so, remain as an offering because the service spins off jobs. Independent consultants typically recommend shedding and dissolving services that are Dogs.

- Question Marks are those services that may garner little interest, but are on the cutting edge of trends, and meet the needs of an audience. At first, these service may generate less revenue than their earnings. They are called Question Marks because in their infancy, it remains questionable whether or not to invest in growth. However, with proper management, Question Marks can often prove to be Stars.
- Stars are services that attract great numbers of users and operate in environments for which there is great growth potential. Since Stars generate substantial income to costs, they should be nurtured with good management and proper investment. Stars attract loyalty and stand apart as signature offerings.

Ideally, organizations have several services that span across the growth–share matrix. The balanced portfolio is comprised of:

- Stars whose high share and high growth assure the future.
- Cash Cows that supply funds for that future growth.
- Question Marks to be converted into Stars with the added funds.

Reducing Risk

The College Board, which designs and administers the Standard Aptitude Test for college admissions, faces great risk to its organization with every test it develops. SATs are part of the admissions process for a majority of the nation's two thousand six hundred eighteen accredited four-year colleges and universities. Those who score poorly can find themselves restricted from schools that best match their abilities. Poor results, moreover, can impact entire communities besides ruining the College Board's image.

Due to the high stakes—the potential to impact student futures—both the IRS and College Board expend enormous resources to ensure fairness. Both organizations rely on a rigorous process for testing and prototyping—seeking points of failure before they occur.

Test Development

Test Development Committees, educators and subject-matter experts decide subject areas to cover. Then, they create a structure for questions such as whether the question sufficiently measures knowledge, skills, and understanding. Is it a fair question to ask of *all* students? Are questions phrased and constructed in a way that students will recognize them as has been taught at high schools? Are some of the criteria used for question structures?

Review Process

Professional test developers write the questions. Then each is thoroughly vetted by representative educational experts. Students are brought in as testers, and answers are statistically tabulated for analysis.

The questions and answers are also reviewed by a

College Board policy committee and a panel from higher education. Additionally, the questions are inserted into official tests, but not scored. Students are aware that some of the questions are under consideration, and are not tallied in their scores.

14 – PROTOTYPING

The Marshall's Revisited

After VRBO took over the financial transactions of its short-term rental vacationers and owners, the Marshalls began to question whether it made sense to continue using the online service. Using the service blueprint to prototype the service operation made it possible to track a typical renter's experience.

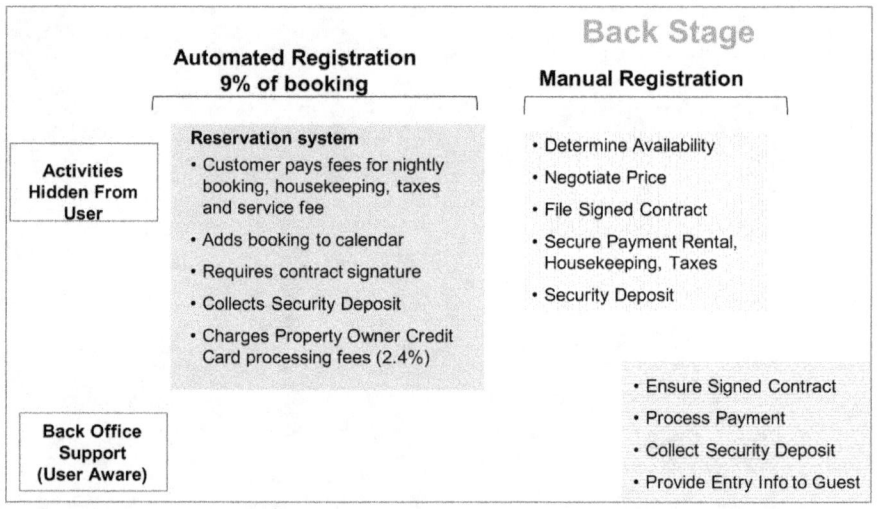

ATTRACTING RENTERS

What the Marshalls discovered was how little they knew or understood of their renters' experiences. While the business had grown steadily during more than ten years, the

Marshalls didn't have any notion of the search terms renters used for their property to appear at the top of VRBO's search engine. As simple as that sounds, the Marshalls, and their friends and family, had over the years tried using the search engine to find the property, with little success. In addition, the Marshalls had yet to book a repeat customer, and still the reviews were outstanding.

THE MARSHALLS VS. VRBO

When VRBO's business model changed, the Marshalls assumed the services that came along with the new charges were simply a waste of money. They reached out to potential renters telling them so, and suggested booking directly with the Marshalls to avoid a 9 percent fee. No takers. And the Marshalls themselves resented VRBO sticking them and all other owners with the 3 percent credit card processing fee that resulted when renters paid VRBO by credit card.

However, after prototyping the entire renter experience the Marshalls discovered VRBO's automation was saving considerable administrative time. With more tweaking, the automation ensured contracts were signed, payments received, and security deposits collected and held in escrow. Other aspects of the Marshalls' business operation were revealed, with opportunities to improve. The Marshalls saw where they could insert touchpoints—to determine a renter's expectations—and another to alert them if the renter's experience was failing, and others for after the experience was complete.

Using the blueprint this way, the Marshalls could appreciate the experience from the renter's viewpoint. But they could also visualize their separate roles in managing the unit, where fail points could occur, and ways to continue improving the renters' experience.

Further Benefits of Prototyping

- Collaboration
    - Visibility-transparency
    - Shared understanding, communicating (the service)
- Learning the service process and mechanics (service system and service operation)
    - Explore service boundaries
- Stretch capabilities—scale
- Point(s) of failure
    - Understanding—sourcing
- Resources, roles, functions, and responsibilities
- Scheduling and timelines
- Qualifying purpose
    - Match to persona(s)
    - Discovering user expectations
    - Evaluate user experiences
- Communications
- Use of touchpoints
- Gathering feedback

FEMA Seeks to Avoid Disaster

When Hurricane Andrew devastated Homestead, Florida in 1992, FEMA was excoriated by media and lawmakers for its slow, uncoordinated response. Yet the Federal Emergency Management Agency had been authorized by Congress to assist local response efforts upon request, and even then, they stayed out of public view.

Nonetheless, lawmakers took to grilling FEMA's director James Lee Witt demanding the agency improves. Witt, a Bill Clinton appointee and one of the more respected FEMA directors, decided the agency's communications need to improve. Improvements to communications would bring more awareness nationally to FEMA's work, better inform disaster victims of available federal services, and bring order to the typical chaos among local officials who often struggle with how to communicate with affected communities.

FEMA, by the way, is always aiding disaster victims somewhere in the nation: from when FEMA arrives on sight, it could be years before an operation is over and temporary FEMA workers clock out or move on to the next disaster.

To satisfy Witt, a team of communications managers and professionals from around the country were gathered atop Mt. Weather, a government outpost located near Winchester, Va., roughly 50 miles from the nation's capital. Mt. Weather is an ideal location for a retreat. In the 1950s, the mountain was hallowed so the entire Congress could relocate and function there in the event of a nuclear attack.

When the team of communications professionals arrived, the facility resembled an abandoned movie set. There were empty parking lots along a perimeter road, a few immaculate barracks, and some isolated bunkers constructed with concrete and cinder blocks lined with a layer of steel, altogether measuring several feet thick.

Above all, the environment offered no distractions and the team set to work. Over the course of two weeks, the group working with FEMA officials devised blueprints for ways to respond with communications given any number of circumstances due to emergencies. They then ran successive drills to prototype the blueprints, looking for points of failure that would prevent FEMA's communications from operating, including the inability of critical people and supplies to get into place.

A few weeks later, FEMA was called upon to respond to tornado damage from a storm that ripped through Arkansas. The tornados leveled several towns to the point where residents could not recognize where their houses once stood. Cars were picked up by the winds and put down inside buildings. Storm paths crisscrossed vast swaths, eliminating everything down to bare earth. Still, in some locations, just yards away from where pavement was ripped away, whole trees were left untouched, with no visible signs of damage even to their leaves.

The disaster provided an ideal trial run for FEMA's new communications plans which involved building tents on site with stations to advise residents where to find shelter and food and how to file insurance claims. Besides helping repair FEMA's reputation, hopefully these changes also helped residents more quickly restore to some degree of normalcy.

15 – MEASURING QUALITY

The shift to a service economy has heighted interest in finding reliable ways to measure the quality of a service. It has already established a successful service depends on satisfying users—delivering a positive, reliable experience outcome. So the search is on for measuring satisfaction.

The origins of reliable user measurements can trace along the lines of what some advertisers refer to as finding the holy grail—the sweet spot between how much to spend on advertising in return for maximum response.

Advertising outlets figure out how much to charge for advertising based on the number of possible "eyeballs." But no matter how much effort and care goes into planning advertising campaigns, there is always an unknown amount of wastage—an uncertain number who are never going to take action. No amount of coverage is going to convince someone to buy dog food if they don't have a dog.

Due to the issue of wastage coupled with ever improved capabilities using digital media to targeting specific individuals, advertisers are getting closer than ever to paying a more precise cost to reach just those targeted consumers at an optimum time in a buying cycle.

Digital media is helping satisfy the desire for better consumer data collection, to more precisely couple actions and activities with behavior, emotion and motivation. As digital media becomes ever more efficient and reliable for gathering insights, more quality services will compete to deliver heightened experiences.

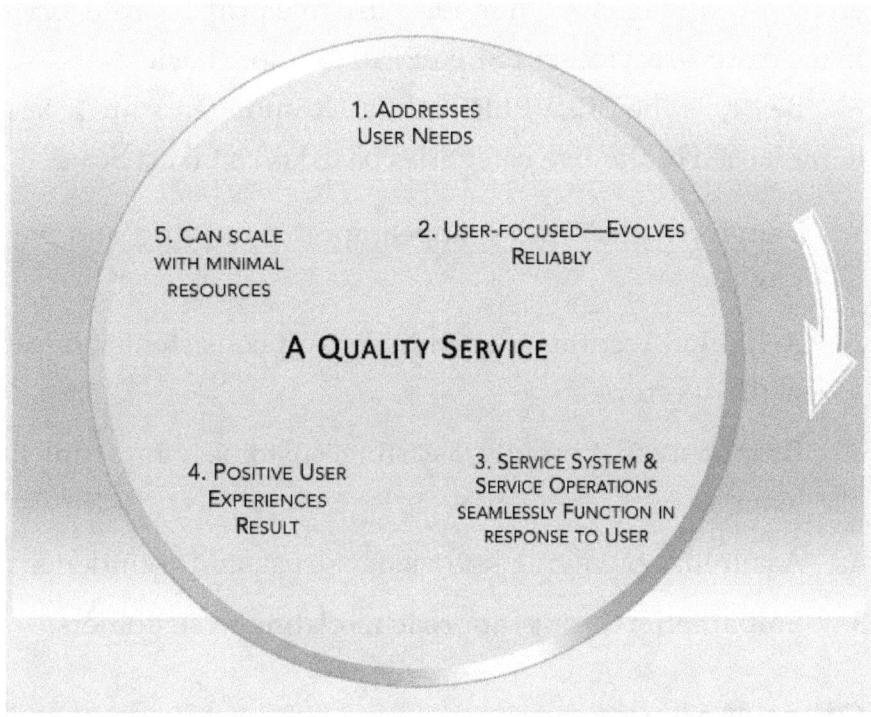

SERVQUAL and SERVPERF Measurements

Small groups of dedicated researchers have for decades been working on ways to measure services. In 1988, one such group, A. Parasurman, Valarie Zeithaml, and Leonard L. Berry, published findings of research based on matching user expectations to service outcomes.

Their model, SERVQUAL is based on forty-four survey questions requiring the skills of a researcher to administer.

Some say it is too unwieldy to be practical, though it is commonly used in financial services. A more feasible alternative is SERVPERF. The major difference is SERVPERF measures quality as an attitude—relying on user decisions rather than on their sentiments. Both models use five primary categories to measure a service, but SERVPERF, is more basic.

Below is the SERVPERF model. Respondents are asked to rank each of the five categories based on a Likert Scale.

1. **Tangible:** Cleanliness, appearance of facilities and employees;

2. **Reliable:** Accurate, dependable, and consistent services without errors.

3. **Responsive**: Promptly assisting customers in a timely manner.

4. **Assured**: Conveying knowledge, trust, and confidence.

5. **Empathetic**: Caring, approach, relating to customers.

Other Measurements

There are less scientific, less rigorous, ways of tackling service measurements than SERVQUAL. Some of them are familiar, and can be combined for greater accuracy. The chart on the next page is an example of some of the qualitative and quantitative measurements most any organization can adopt.

But first, executives must understand the objectives for research gathering, the intent and purpose for its use. The purpose will drive the urgency and methods for data collection and naturally lead to deciding which data is most valuable and may require additional resources to gather.

Already, we have discussed several purposes for research, including to uncover motivation and potential obstacles used to improve services, and also, the importance of research gathering for personas and the qualitative and quantitative gathering for plotting journey maps.

Info Gathering	Purpose	How	What
NPS SCORE	**Priority 1:** Segment 'Promoters' for high-touch focus. **Priority 2:** Segment 'Passives' to attempt conversion to Promoter.	Survey question: "Would you recommend . . . to others?	Quantitative - numeric scoring (Likert Scale)
PERSONAS	Audience segmentation. Used to engage, attract, communicate and motivate ideal audience segments.	Create profiles of target audience groups (i.e. millennials); use research to learn interests, traits, and behaviors.	Qualitative (open-ended, results uncertain)
TOUCHPOINTS	*For Feedback: General rule --* • Qualitative (open-ended questions) to learn problems and failures. • Quantitative (numeric) to verify findings. • Observations to discover user interactions. (see Journeymaps)	Net Promoter Score (NPS)	Mix of quantitative-qualitative-observation.

Also, here are some other satisfaction measurements, a borrowed web application design, including a Word Tool. The one below has been adopted from Hilary Palmén's article, "How Was It for You? Helping People Describe Their Experiences," including adjectives from the website—In the Mood? 100 Ways to Describe How You Feel. Some may find these adjectives useful for questionnaires or touchpoints.

Palmén says the tool has helped her uncover user emotions that might lead to motivation. She said she used the tool, as a touchpoint to measure users' website experiences, using drop-down menus. "The inspiration," she said, "originates from a psychology test in which respondents select descriptive words to describe experiences. The words can be used to drill down and capture nuances."

Whichever method used, the greater number of responses provide more accuracy. With large populations, researchers use statistics to sample.

Word	Definition
acceptable	Generally approved or compelling recognition
amazed	Fiilled with the emotional impact of overwhelming surprise
amused	Pleasantly occupied
apathetic	Showing little or no emotion or animation
astonished	Filled with the emotional impact of overwhelming surprise
aversion	A feeling of intense dislike
avoidance	Deliberately avoiding
awed	Inspired by a feeling of fearful wonderment or reference
awful	Exceptionally bad or displeasing
boring	Tired of the world
confused	Unable to think with clarity or act intelligently
critical	Marked by a tendency to find and call attention to flaw
detestable	Offensive to the mind
disappointed	Sadly unsuccessful
disapproving	Expressing or manifesting disapproval
disillusioned	Freed from false ideas

Word	Definition
dismayed	Struck with fear, dread, or consternation
eager	Having or showing keep interest or intense desire
ecstatic	Feeling great rapture or delight
empty	Void of emotion
energetic	Possessing or displaying forceful exertion
enraged	Marked by extreme anger
excited	In an aroused state
frustrated	Disappointingly unsuccessful
fulfilled	Completed to perfection
hesitant	Unable to act or decide quickly or firmly
hopeful	Having or manifesting optimism
hostile	Characterized by enmity or ill will
ignored	Disregarded
important	Of great significance or value
inadequate	Not sufficient to meet a need
indifferent	Marked by a lack of interest
inferior	Of low quality
infuriated	Marked by extreme anger
insignificant	Of little importance or influence or power; of minor status or surpassing excellence
interested	Showing curiosity or fascination or concern
irritated	Aroused to impatience or anger
judgmental	Depending on assessing a person or situation or event
open	Straightforward and direct without reserve or secretiveness
optimistic	Hopeful that the best will happen in the future
overwhelmed	Overcome, as with emotions or perceptual stimuli
perplexed	Full of difficulty or confusion or bewilderment

Word	Definition
powerful	Having great force or effect
powerless	Lacking power
proud	Feeling self-respect, self-esteem, or self-importance
provocative	Serving or tending to excite or stimulate
rejected	Rebuffed (by a lover) without warning
sarcastic	Expressing or expressive of ridicule that wounds
sensitive	Responsive to physical stimuli
shocked	Struck with fear, dread, or surprise
skeptical	Marked by or given to doubt
suspicious	Openly distrustful and unwilling to confide
worthless	Lacking in usefulness or value

REFERENCES

Mohd, A., Dr., Mohammad Al Ghaswyneh, O., Dr., & Albkour, A. (2013). SERVQUAL and SERVPERF: A Review of Measures in Services Marketing Research. Global Journal of Management and Business Research Marketing,13(6), 1. 0st ser., 65-76. Retrieved February 15, 2018, from

https://www.google.com/search?q=SERVQUAL and SERVPERF%3A A Review of Measures in Services Marketing Research&oq=SERVQUAL and SERVPERF%3A A Review of Measures in Services Marketing Research&aqs=chrome..69i57j69i60l2.1268j0j1&sourceid=chrome&ie=UTF-8.

Chapter VII
Avoiding Failure

"Even though services fail because of human incompetence, drawing a bead on this target obscures the underlying cause—the lack of systematic method for design and control."

G. Lynn Shostack
Designing Services That Deliver

16 – THE NATURE OF FAILURE

I have yet to see a direct correlation between poor customer service and service failure. Yet there seems no shortage of those who would lead us to believe poor customer service results in service demise.

Take for example this recent book title, *Service Failure, The Real Reasons Employees Struggle with Customer Service and What You Can Do About It.* For all this book's possible merits, along with hundreds of other writings on this topic—it defies logic that poor customer service causes services to fail.

For one, customer service is immeasurably vague as a fault. Two: to remedy poor customer service with a one-size-fits-all solution ignores the wide variety of services and situations; most share no similarity. And three, many services with poor service reputations still have ascended to market leadership.

It is more true, however, that services succeed or fail based on whether and how they meet the needs of users. As such, no matter how well-thought through these home-brewed remedies are for improving customer service in and of themselves, they will not rescue a service from failing.

The Common Causes for Services to Fail

1. The Service fails to meet users' needs and expectations: Users choose not to participate, or worse, bail out before the service experience concludes.

2. Services fail to meet the needs of an organization:

    a. The primary objective of the service is not met.

    b. A trade-off (balance) between costs and benefits fail to materialize. The organization spends too much on resources (manpower or technology) for return.

    c. The service takes too long to unfold.

For all intents and purposes, the discussion could end here. The use of a service blueprint is likely to result in a diagnosis and remedy. Often, executives will find gaps in how a service unfolds.

Other Signs of Services Failing

1. Users are confused about the purpose and the ultimate benefit of using a service. The underlying reason is failing to create and convey a valid expectation. The results and corrections lay with:

    a. Poor persona insights.

    b. Misleading or confusing communications through touchpoints.

    c. The communications by others, including staff, mis-representing a service and its benefit(s).

2. Users expressing frustration with a service as it unfolds, is due to:

    a. Providers are not fully engaged in the success or outcome of a service.

    b. The functional staff is disconnected from each other unaware of purpose for the service, or possibly are unable to recognize or appreciate their roles for moving the service forward.

    c. Executives and managers fail to set adequate goals.

    d. The service operation (frontstage and backstage) is missing sufficient standard procedures.

3. Service "quality" is wanting. Signs of trouble appear from, and are resolved through:

    a. Technical aspects of the service that don't measure up.

    b. Roles and responsibilities conflict or are ambiguous.

    c. Poorly trained staff, or poor functional alignment to individual skills.

    d. Inadequate minimum standards.

    e. Improper management-supervision.

4. Unclear communications establishing user expectations are wanting due to:

a. Poor internal communications and proper handoffs.
b. Lacking context for communicating with users.
c. Conflicting standards, policies, and procedures.
d. Overpromising and under delivering the intended service outcome.

Next is guidance on how to avoid failures from occurring.

17 – PREVENTING FAILURE

Services are designed in layers, one element on top of another, in a sequence of stages. Each stage should be guided by Service Design practices including overall approach, process, methods, and tools. Following each process also requires teams of individuals with insights into the organization and experience and skills for their assigned functions and tasks.

Even following Service Design practices, challenges emerge. The following are some of the pitfalls:

Excluding Stakeholders' Input

Successful services require user involvement to validate needs and determine the shape of the result. Ignoring this aspect of Service Design risks designing a poor quality service.

If You Don't Set Expectations, Others Will

"Expectations can be the cause of the failure, not the other way around," Edward Yourdon, wrote in *Managing the System Life Cycle.* "Perception can be more important than reality. And make sure to explain ahead any problems users might face." Failure to set expectations is against one of the principles of Service Design.

Avoid the Cheap Way Out

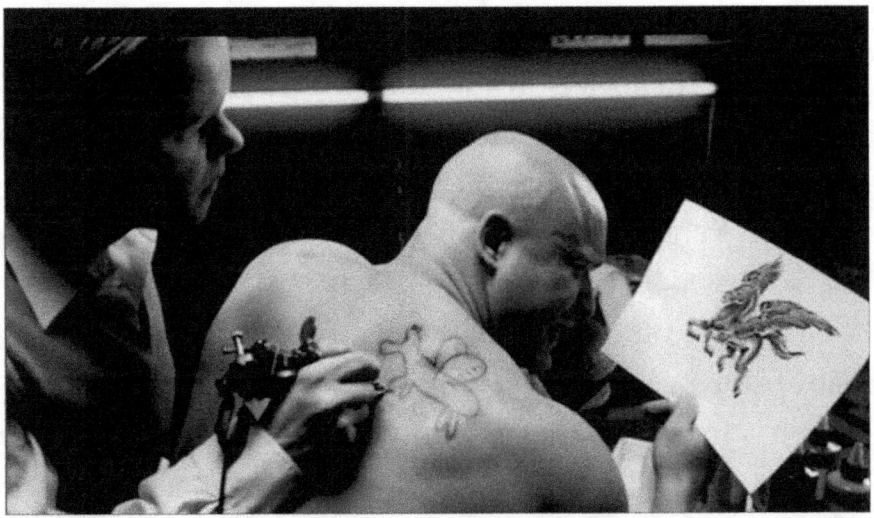

Cable Company Loses Customer Connection

A cable company in our DC area was regulated by the local government, proscribed in the regulations of the Federal Communications Commission.

For nearly two decades, the privately-held "ACME" company was required to share its finances publicly, and to request approval of rate increases. A county government office was set aside for managing ACME which also scrutinized its customer service. ACME was forced to report monthly how long it took to respond to outages along with consumer complaints—including how long customers waited on the phone for someone from ACME's customer support to answer. The government took its managing authority as one of its constituent hallmarks. As a result, ACME had very little control in the monopolistic environment in which they were the only cable service carriers.

During a tour to their call center during that time, the CEO proudly showed off a sports complex-sized LED display with a sweep of his hand. The board showed which phone lines were receiving customer calls, the time from when they called in to how soon the call was picked up, and how long the call lasted. However, the CEO's overall message was how the county's office for cable regulation prevented his company from investing into technologies that would benefit customers. And further, that county's requirements tipped the balance away from ACME earning profits that matched the industry.

Some years later, a competitor entered the county, and the county's jurisdiction to regulate the cable utility came to an end. From then on, the response times for customer support phone calls went up dramatically, and appointments for repairs went from within the next two days, to within the next two weeks. Additionally, the number outages increased, which ACME said was due to outdated equipment from the years of regulation.

In any event, many former ACME customers left and signed up for the competitor's cable service. Once the competitor had built up its customer base, it devoted its resources to converting them into promoters, and rewarding promoters through rates and services.

Had I been able to advise ACME, I would have invested resources into my subscribers and asked them about their experiences and expectations. Instead, ACME took the easy route—perhaps because they were given their freedom from regulation, they failed to tackle on their own the challenges the county cable office faced among constituents. From others' perspectives, ACME looked to cash in, ignoring the principles of Service Design: Long-term benefits accruing for those who build their service around the user.

Over Confidence Leads to Incompetency

These days, most any service requires sufficient, working technology. Hence successful services require skills that include someone to serve as a leader. The individual must be qualified with experiences that piece together the technical components of a service. Absent this role, the chances increase that a service will not operate smoothly. It is likely the service won't work as expected, if at all.

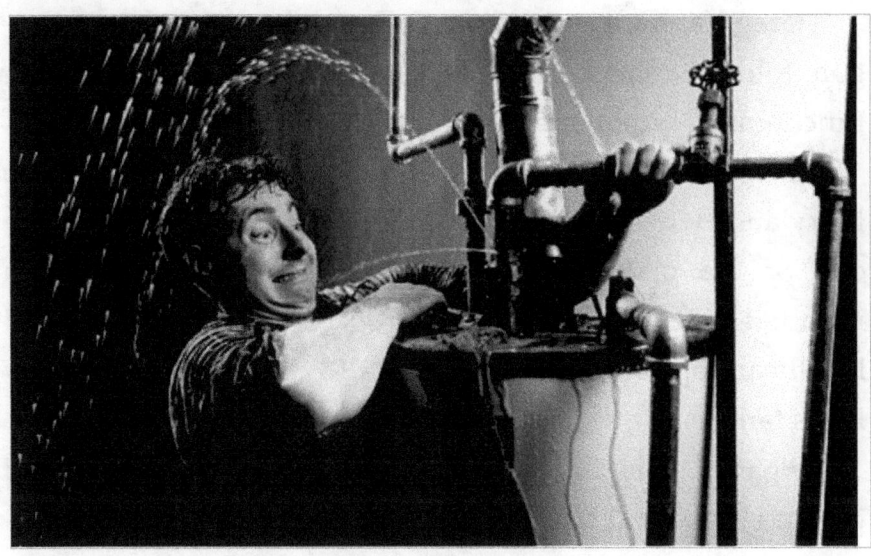

Any Empathy for Failing Healthcare Rollout?

Regardless of your political position on the Affordable Care Act (Obamacare)—it wasn't the scope or complexity that proved the biggest obstacle. It was the technology.

Technical problems are among the most common ways services fail, according to a J. D. Power Shopper-Satisfaction Survey in 2014. "No doubt that ensuring a technologically error-free experience... will be most impactful," said Rick Johnson, senior director of the healthcare practice at J. D. Power.

After the disastrous rollout, Capitol Hill lawmakers wanted to know why some states managed to enroll only a few tens of thousands enrollees, despite the fact that federal grants totaled hundreds of millions of dollars for the effort to succeed.

"Our rollout was rocky," Scott Leitz testified, interim chief executive of the Minnesota exchange. "Our launch was plagued by software errors and technical glitches."

Greg Van Pelt, an adviser to Gov. John Kitzhaber of Oregon, told lawmakers the state's website was "only partially functioning" when open enrollment commenced.

But by any measure, the worst failure belonged to Maryland, whose exchange "immediately crashed" on day one of the open enrollment period, the Baltimore Sun reported. The failure was captured on national news, and healthcare opponents jumped on it to demonstrate the new law's failure.

Against this backdrop, the federal government had granted Maryland two hundred eighty-million dollars to automate the enrollment process, among the highest amounts awarded to states. Plus, President Obama had been selling his program around the country telling state leaders that Maryland was going to blaze the example for a smooth rollout.

But on October 1, the enrollment start date, Maryland's system crashed unable to accommodate the numbers of residents who tried to apply. Six months later and with many date extensions, just twenty-five percent of the state's population were enrolled, forcing the state to hire teams of individuals to take applicant information over the phone.

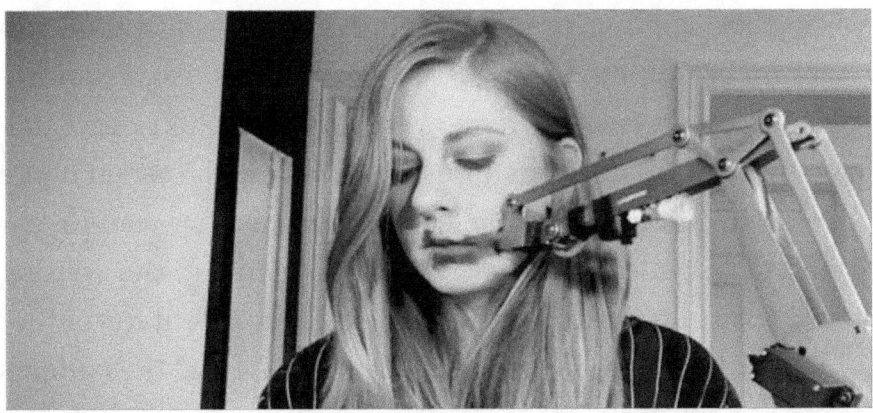

The failure was due in part from failing to test the system. But the larger problem, it turns out, was because the designated technical lead had no technical expertise. Just days before the launch, the manager responsible for overseeing the state's healthcare program walked into the IT office and found it empty, as reported in the Baltimore Sun. "Tonight, I am begging. I don't know how else to say it: we have got to make this a reality," she wrote in an email sent to the IT contractors.

Maryland's state leaders paid the price. During the next election, the majority of the Democratic state voters elected an unknown Republican as their governor, rejecting Lt. Gov. Anthony Brown who had said at the launch of his campaign a year earlier that he wanted to be known for rolling out the new federal healthcare program. And until the system crashed, he was leading in the polls.

Mistrust is Infectious

Shelly Granholm, an emergency-care nurse at a large urban hospital walked into the waiting room on her way to clock in for her shift—and was surprised and disappointment to find the waiting room rearranged and a new process in place for admitting patients.

The triage desk—where nurses assess patients and discuss sensitive medical histories—was now in the center of the crowded waiting room, just feet away from other waiting patients. And patients who were once returned to the waiting room after initial triage assessment were now sent to another waiting room where a group of doctors reviewed the patients for treatment decisions.

The changes were precipitated by hospital administrators who, among themselves, came up with a new process to move patients through the system—designed to improve speed and efficiency. However, administrators moved forward without emergency medical staff input.

The new procedure had been in planning for months, and Granholm vaguely remembers an email on the topic, or perhaps mentioning it during a staff meeting.

True, the emergency room is often in chaos as it is one of the busiest hospitals in the nation. Yet doctors and nurses had worked with their situation and had an informal process in place. As a result, wait times had indeed been reduced as much as by one-half, even while the numbers of patients were increasing. In a department with just thirty-eight beds, the staff could accommodate one hundred patients at a time. However, the administrator's new process put the entire operation into uncertainty.

The administrators, overall, were guilty of violating many principles of good management. Consequently, their heavy-handed action resulted in uneven staff workloads, causing patients to wait longer.

Granholm left work that day with a lot of bitter feelings: the emergency staff had not even been asked if there was a problem needing fixing, nor asked for feedback or participation in the new process. "This will never work," she said.

And whether or not she is correct is an unknown. However, having been excluded from the process almost guarantees Granholm and her colleagues won't help the new process succeed.

Epilog

Some look to Service Design to make ever larger impacts to our lives, including improvements to transportation, healthcare delivery, and solutions to climate change.

~ ~ ~

In Europe, service designers have informed engineers on how to create rider experiences and have developed devices and apps for riders to plan routes, determine fares, and purchase tickets—even before they step out of their house. Also, navigation has improved by installing automated kiosks and online help desks, plus new signage using symbols instead of language text. The design of platforms, too, was made so riders could more easily access other modes of travel.

These improvements needed to take into consideration those riders coming and going from and to different countries, and whose citizens were familiar with their own transportation systems. Many of Europe's inner-city rail and bus lines, for instance, trust passengers to buy tickets on the honor system, and were only shown when the random inspector asks.

Europe was developed long before any consideration of cars or sidewalks, and there isn't enough room for every city resident to own a car. So public transportation has become part of everyday life—critical to getting anywhere: from across town, to across the country, to across Europe. Due to the agreement forming the European Union, workers now have access to jobs across borders, providing they can reach them. By helping integrate the people-part of the transportations systems, service designers have had to be cognizant of what riders have grown accustomed to, and to figure out how to make transitions to new ways smooth—which is making them easily understood.

Both systems engineers and service designers have been part of bringing to fruition transportation systems of the future. These will be along the lines of implementing a JourneyMap essentially integrating travel from door to door. So for instance, a passenger's journey begins from considering the trip, to planning and purchasing tickets, to getting picked up by an on-demand ride, to a transportation hub, and so on until passengers reach their destination. This journey could include roundtrip, as well. To make this real will involve a mobile application that probably uses an API (Application Program Interface) to connect with other applications for using capabilities for planning and organizing an optimum route—by cost, time, distance, etc.—then having the ability to purchase tickets for the entire journey. Those tickets would reside on the mobile application to pass through ticket gates, or for conductors to scan. Also, the mobile application would have navigation with real time directions, instructions, and updates toward completing the journey.

Healthcare Delivered on Your Terms

Service design is playing a role for how we receive healthcare, one that is based on preventing illnesses with treatments tailored to each individual. This is compared to our current system that has, for all of the millennial, been based on treating illness.

"We are on the cusp of some of the greatest opportunities for transformation in diagnosis, treatment, and disease prevention," president and CEO of Boston Children's Hospital, Sandra L. Fenwick, told Forbes' online magazine.

Until now, advancements in healthcare have been based on trial and error through graduated studies that take place over years if not decades. Medical treatments derive from statistics, percentages, likelihoods, and probabilities since no two individuals react the same.

From a longer-lens perspective, anyone who has practiced medicine has looked to heal the sick with remedies known and available. But we have advanced to the point of being able to diagnose someone before they become ill, Kan S. Lee, Ph.D., said, a retired researcher from the National Institutes of Health based just outside of Washington, D.C. Using DNA, we currently can pinpoint someone's genes that cause specific illnesses or maladies. But the advancements are moving us toward capabilities for mapping each individual's entire DNA for any variety of illnesses. This will allow practitioners to shift focus toward more preventive care.

"As for patients, this shift will require regular testing with results leading to individual prevention plans, and likely a regimen of medicines, vitamins, and devices," Dr. Lee said. All of which will require orchestrating providers, practitioners, and the patients themselves—an outcome requiring service design. No other practice can tie together the separate aspects required for preventive care and meeting overall needs—including cost, speed, and organization.

"Personalized care planning when combined with behavioral economic principles drives engagement," Paul Kusserow, president and CEO of Amedisys Home Health & Hospice, said. "I think eighty percent of all health care could be cured or avoided if people changed their behaviors and habits. Once people are responsible for, and own, their care management and compliance, they can positively impact their own health."

Mitigating Disaster

On May 22, 2011 at suppertime, a 230-mph tornado as wide as a mile across, skipped across Joplin, MO, a city of just more than fifty-thousand residents. The storm obliterated schools, businesses, and government buildings leaving piles of rubble and broad scars.

This was the third time in forty years that a deadly tornado struck Joplin. This time, however, city leaders and institutions came together to address resiliency—ways to try and protect their city against future storms, and a methodical approach to rebuilding. Their plans were rooted in investing resources for prevention and restoration for schools and businesses, in that priority order.

Nowadays, dozens of communities across the United States have adopted resiliency plans, their leaders knowing that they will inevitably face impacts due to climate change. Areas most at risk include: areas along the coasts susceptible to flooding; areas where hurricanes have been recorded; areas that lie along the paths of tornados, and areas prone to ever increasing dry spells. In fact, the National Academy of Sciences and others have recommended city leaders in these areas to specifically identify the risks and devise structural and non-structural ways to mitigate them.

These plans require satisfying the needs of residents, which most certainly will require affording higher taxes. Some city leaders have turned to service design demand models for informing and educating residents. Through evolving messages of a demand model, the initial aim would be to create awareness among residents. The city leaders would want to educate residents about possible different approaches toward resiliency, follow proposed methods to measure progress. Along with the messages, city leaders should plan for open forums as a way to involve residents: they then become advocates, or in the lexicon of Service Design—they are the loyalists.

Just like transportation or healthcare, climate change mitigation is designed around users, and the interactions between them and the service. Along these lines, the approach of service design is vital to managing those services. For one, Service Design will ensure providers are responsive to the needs of users. For two, through prototyping, services are more reliable. And three, the services will continue improving with user feedback and measurement.

Glossary

A SERVICE

The perception and expectations of the output and delivery, including those of the members' staff, shareholders, and vendors.

AN EXPERIENCE

The process or fact of personally observing, encountering, or undergoing something, generally as they occur over the course of time. Knowledge or practical wisdom gained from what one has observed, encountered, or undergone.

CONTEXT

The specific frame in which the service takes place. Exploring and defining the context means setting the boundaries and defining the opportunities.

CUSTOMER JOURNEY MAP

An oriented graph describing the journey of members, represented by Touchpoints and characterizing the interaction with the service. In this kind of visualization, the interaction is described step by step as in the classical service Blueprint.

ENVISIONING

Represents the service idea using visuals representing the components of the service, including physical elements, interaction modalities, logical links and temporal sequences.

INTERACTION

The experience of the member and organization at the same juncture. This requires identifying the Touchpoints and choices: devices used, staff behaviors, and resulting activities.

METHODOLOGY

A set or system of tools, principles, and rules for regulating a given discipline.

MODELS

In the practice of service design, models are preliminary works and constructions—such as the demand or behavior models—to plan operations of the service. Constructions can be tested.

NARRATIVES

A collection of events that tell a story, true or not. They appear in an order and are recounted through telling, representing, or writing.

OFFERING

Defined by the benefits of using a service—the performance expected.

PROCESS

A systematic series of actions directed to an end goal.

LEADS

Expertise required for the development of the service idea. Specifically qualified to engage target audiences from beginning to service expectation. Most often, these are individuals with knowledge of marketing, research and analysis, technology, change management and training, and organizational design—covering business, technology, and social sciences.

SERVICE OPERATION

Refers to arranging separate components with available resources—people and technology—into desired outputs (satisfied members).

SERVICE STAFF

People involved in the final delivery of the service, including front stage operators where direct interactions occur, to operators in the back stage, supporting the activities and interactions occurring on the front stage.

SERVICE SYSTEM

Process, workflows to maintain quality (delivery standards).

STAKEHOLDERS

Persons, groups or organizations with direct or indirect organizational involvement, those who can affect or be affected by an organization's actions. Stanford research institute defined stakeholders as "groups without whose support the organization would cease to exist." A broader definition in use: anyone with a legitimate interest in a project or entity.

SYSTEM

Describing the system is to identify the main figures involved, the relations among them, and their activities and aims in taking part in the service process.

PROTOTYPING

To experience aspects of a service idea with customers, stakeholders, or professionals, so solutions can be tested prior to launch.

TOOLS

Exercises and templates to carry out an operation used for service design, such as journey maps, Touchpoints and Blueprints.

USERS

People, customers, members, and consumers making use of a service. Any person, organization, or system that uses a service provided by others is a user.

About the Author

Steven is both an award-winning business writer, with multiple prizes, and a Service Designer—who has built and improved programs and services across various industries.

During his 30-plus years' career, he has launched multiple programs for business and industry, non-profits, and government. Among them include new global services for Booz Allen Hamilton; a philanthropic portal and shared content for United Jewish Communities, a national software application development training program for National Industries for the Blind; and participating in building a national training and jobs database for the Department of Labor and a rapid response disaster program for the Federal Emergency Management Agency.

He has served as advisor to multiple senior-level executives, including senior presidential appointees at the Department of Defense and Department of Transportation, and at Booz Allen Hamilton as a chief of staff.

Steven has an MBA with a concentration in Marketing Sciences from Johns Hopkins University; an M.A. in Journalism and Public Affairs from American University; and a B.A. in International Relations and Communications from Syracuse University.

Additionally, Steven was an early International Baccalaureate graduate from the International School of Geneva,

Switzerland.

www.ingramcontent.com/pod-product-compliance
Lightning Source LLC
Chambersburg PA
CBHW070229180526
45158CB00001BA/189